— THE —
NINETEENTH YEAR

Published 2012.

Printed in the United States of America.

ISBN: 978-1-59571-799-3
Library of Congress Control Number: 2012937534

Designed and published by

Word Association Publishers
205 Fifth Avenue
Tarentum, Pennsylvania 15084

www.wordassociation.com
1.800.827.7903

— THE —
NINETEENTH YEAR

A Sweet Summer with the Pittsburgh Pirates

MICHAEL E. LOWENSTEIN

WORD ASSOCIATION PUBLISHERS
www.wordassociation.com
1.800.827.7903

To Andee. For everything.

Every family should have one picture that captures all of its hopes and dreams. This is ours.

Every family should have one picture that captures hopes and dreams. This is ours:

PART ONE

CHAPTER ONE

HEARTBREAK

The Pittsburgh Pirates entered the ninth inning of the seventh game of the 1992 National League playoffs with a two-to-nothing lead over the Atlanta Braves. The Pirates had made the playoffs three years in a row. They had lost the other two. It was a big night and my wife Andee and I let our three young children, Lauren, Rachel and David, ages eight, six and four, stay up to watch. One of them, Lauren, went the distance.

Doug Drabek was the Pirates' pitcher. He was their ace. In the biggest game of his career, Drabek had been masterful for eight innings. With a little luck and a little help, he might have been masterful for nine. But after defensive sub Cecil Espy could not handle a difficult fly he might have caught, a bobbled grounder by the usually reliable second baseman Jośe Lind, and a four-pitch walk to former Pirate Sid Bream, Drabek's night, and in fact his Pirate career, was over.

People often forget how close the Pirates came to getting out of that ninth inning. Stan Belinda came in and got two outs and the Bucs still held a 2-1 lead. Down to their last out, with runners on second and third, the Braves sent up Francisco Cabrera, who had three hits the whole season. There are people, some of them on the Pirates, who will go to their graves believing that the strike zone was narrowed on Stan Belinda that night. Whether that was true or not, Cabrera smacked a solid single to left, Bream, who may have been the slowest player in baseball, lumbered home from second base with the winning run an instant ahead of the just-wide throw, and it was done.

As the Braves mobbed Bream and Cabrera, Lauren burst into tears. A few minutes later, CBS conducted one of those hard interviews with Pirate Manager Jim Leyland. Leyland rose to the occasion with dignity and grace, and what he said spoke directly to our daughter: This is a lesson for all you kids out there. You don't always win.

Our children are grown now. They have learned this lesson well. In the next eighteen years, they never saw another Pirate team with a winning record.

CHAPTER TWO

EIGHTEEN YEARS

In fact, the Pirates' eighteen-year losing streak was the longest in the history of American professional sports. This would be a better story if I said we lived and died with each of those eighteen miserable seasons. But it wouldn't be true. Are you out of your mind?

Truth be told, we mostly moved on. There was nothing else you could do. But it's a long summer. In a time of life when I let go of a lot of things, I never completely let go of the Pittsburgh Pirates.

I am not sure why. The Pirates were stuck at the bottom of baseball and there didn't seem to be anything they could do about it. This was an era in which some teams would spend five times as much for players as other teams. A time when virtually any good player the Pirates developed soon would be gone. Baseball was broken, and nowhere was it more broken than in Pittsburgh.

Yet the Pirates could scarcely complain. I need to be careful about this because for much of this period I was, of all things, an owner. Our law firm had been one of several local companies who pitched in to keep the team from leaving town and, when we divided our share, I bought my tiny little piece. We had no real say—certainly I didn't—and rightly so. It was a civic duty. Let me just say it this way. The ownership group of which I was a microscopic part saved baseball in Pittsburgh and they also built one of the most beautiful stadiums that anyone ever built. But in an era when small market management had to be better, a lot better, they were not better. They did not invent Moneyball. They did their best but they did not have a good enough plan.

And when you lose for eighteen years in a row, nobody wants to hear it.

CHAPTER THREE

THE IMPOSSIBLE PIRATES

It wasn't always that way...

In 1962, when I was five years old, I used to listen to a wonderful record called "The Impossible Pirates." It told the history of the Pirates, the World Championship teams of 1909 and 1925, and the thirty-five year drought until the World Series of 1960, when the Pirates lost games by 16-3, 12-0 and 10-0 yet somehow found a way to win the only World Series ever to end with a home run in the seventh game. Each year, to this day, hundreds of people gather at the small preserved portion of the left field wall of long-ago demolished Forbes Field on October 13 at one o'clock in the afternoon to listen to the radio broadcast of that seventh game, culminating every year at 3:36 p.m., the exact moment of Bill Mazeroski's timeless blast over that wall and into Schenley Park.

In the 1960s, for me and just about everyone I knew, the Pirates were a part of the rhythms of a thousand spring and summer nights. More than anything, it was Bob Prince, the Gunner, backed by his sidekicks, first Jim Woods, the Possum, and later the giant and gentle-souled Nellie King. Bob Prince was the kind of play-by-play announcer who doesn't exist anymore. He was an unabashed homer, a legendary carouser, and he was not always the most credible. But he made the game exciting and he made you care, and they have never come close to replacing him.

In 1975, after twenty-seven years, Bob Prince was unceremoniously fired to a great public outcry. Ten years later, in an unspoken act of apology, the Pirates brought back a frail and raspy Bob Prince to announce the fourth inning of a game between the Pirates and the Los Angeles Dodgers. The last-place Pirates scored nine runs in that fourth inning and, a month later, Bob Prince died.

For a decade after the 1960 World Championship, the Pirates were in the middle. They did have one magical summer, in 1966, the year of the Green Weenie and a classic three-team pennant race between the Dodgers of Koufax, the Giants of Mays and the Pirates of Clemente. But it was not until the 1970s, in a new venue, Three Rivers Stadium, in the round, cookie-cutter style of the era (already past and not lamented), that the Pirates hit stride.

In the 1970s, the Pirates won two world championships and four other division titles. It was the decade of "The Lumber Company" and "The Family." But the team of teams, at least for me, was in 1971, for reasons that will be explained.

There was much to love about the Pittsburgh Pirates of 1971. They had a Hall of Fame bomber in the prime of his career, Willie Stargell. A group of excellent young hitters who had come up together in the late 1960s. A good if not great pitching staff, led by Steve Blass along with Dock Ellis, who claimed to have once pitched a no-hitter on LSD and to have worn curlers on the mound and who started the All-Star Game that year in Detroit and gave up a home run to Reggie Jackson that may not have landed yet.

Above all there was Roberto Clemente. The Great One. Thirty-seven years old and not an ounce of fat on him. A year and a half later, he would be dead. In the summer of 1971, I saw Roberto Clemente play baseball day after day. Anything that can be done on a baseball field he did that summer, and then, in the 1971 World Series for which he always will be remembered, he did all of them at once. There are people I hear from time to time who would exclude Roberto Clemente from the pantheon of the greatest baseball players. Those people are wrong.

The Pirates' last World Championship came at the end of the 1970s. Most of the stars of 1971 were gone, but Willie Stargell was still there, a grand old man by then but much more than that. In fact, in 1979, he was the co-MVP of the regular season, the MVP of the playoffs and the MVP of the World Series. Stargell was joined by another player who could have gone to the Hall of Fame, although he never will. Dave Parker, six feet five and 235 pounds, with the speed of a running back. He was known as the Cobra and he also had a little Muhammad Ali in him, including his famous if unfulfilled guaranty that "when the leaves turn brown, I will be wearing the Triple Crown."

Dave Parker was a great player for the Pirates in 1979. In 1978, he was the best baseball player on the planet. The stunning and sadly forgotten comeback he led from eleven and a half games back in August 1978 fell just short. But not before Parker led them to a dramatic doubleheader sweep over the Phillies on the last Friday night of the season, news excitedly reported to me at law school just before midnight from a pay phone at Three Rivers Stadium by the girl who then was my new girlfriend and now is my wife of twenty-eight years. The Bucs did not quite make it in 1978 but they set the stage for "The Family" in 1979—and for mine too.

1979 was a watershed year for the Pirates, and also for Pittsburgh, which, it turned out, was looking down the barrel of a devastating collapse of the steel industry that would shake and permanently change the region. For the Pirates and their fans, the 1980s were as trying as the 1970s had been thrilling. During a disastrous period in the mid-1980s, a proud franchise imploded on the field; Pittsburgh hosted an infamous federal drug trial that tarnished the name of many of baseball's most beloved players, including Stargell, and even more so Parker; and the Pirates came perilously close to leaving town.

But, by the end of the decade, the franchise had been saved—by the first of two community efforts, an oddball yet strangely gifted general manager named Syd Thrift, a career minor leaguer in Leyland in his first manager job, and a group of superb young players. One of them turned out to be one of the greatest players who has ever played baseball who, for his trouble—including MVP seasons for the Pirates in 1990 and 1992—quickly became and remains, eighteen years later, by far the most despised athlete in the history of Pittsburgh.

All in all, by 1992, my lifetime as a Pirate fan had been blessed. Three World Championships, each won in dramatic fashion. Seven other division championships. Clemente. Mazeroski. Stargell. Parker. Bonds.

But nothing in life is free. It was time to pay up.

CHAPTER FOUR

THE LOST GENERATION

Every season had some reason to believe and most had at least a small arc of accomplishment. Only the broad sweep of eighteen years reveals the full masterpiece of failure.

Not surprisingly, the Pirates went through five different managers during this time, plus an interim manager or two. First to go, after the 1996 season, was Jim Leyland, hero of the early 1990s, and the only one of the five to leave by choice. Leyland was a born leader and he was an excellent manager in Pittsburgh and since. He was worn down by the losing and by 1996 he looked like the oldest fifty-three-year-old man I had ever seen. That partly excused his abandoning Pittsburgh in a very dark hour, but only partly.

Next up were two of Leyland's coaches. Gene Lamont lasted four years, including 1997, his first year, when a confluence of mediocrity in the Central Division of the National League enabled a Pirate team appropriately dubbed The Freak Show not only to approach the holy grail of the .500 mark but also somehow threaten to make the playoffs, only to fall back in the final week. But the Pirates had not fallen far enough by the late 1990s for people to appreciate the 78- and 79-win seasons Lamont delivered.

After that came Lloyd McClendon, who in five years never won more than 75. McClendon did, however, have a redeeming quality—a fighting spirit on behalf of his team, which would erupt every once in awhile, including the night of a memorable argument when he pulled first base out of the ground and walked away with it. There have been many, many times since when our reaction to a half-hearted effort was that "at least if Lloyd was here he would walk away with first base."

After McClendon walked the plank in 2005, the Pirates turned to Jim Tracy, who had managed the Los Angeles Dodgers to the playoffs in 2004 before falling out of favor. Let me say here that as a general matter I try to see the good in people, at least in watching sports, on the theory that I have more than enough people in real life to make me miserable. I never met Jim Tracy and he might in fact be a wonderful man. But, fairly or not, I instantly disliked Jim Tracy the first time I heard him speak and he never did anything in his two years here that made me change my mind. As far as I was concerned, he was the worst kind of leader, the kind who took the credit when they won and criticized the players when they lost.

Jim Tracy left after the 2007 season; a new management team brought in John Russell. Known for his remarkably flat affect and stoic demeanor, Russell never really had a chance. In some ways he was the right manager for this team. At least publicly, he was utterly unflappable in loss after loss, of which there were 299 in his three years. He did not ruin the promising young players the Pirates were trying to develop. But if Russell was not the problem he certainly was not the solution.

****

These five managers worked for three different owners. Through the 1995 season the Pirates were owned by a consortium of local companies. In 1996 they were sold to a group led by Kevin McClatchy, a young man who loved baseball, from a family that owned newspapers. Most recently, the group has been controlled by the Nutting family, another family in the newspaper business that was a key part of keeping the Pirates in Pittsburgh.

Many people in Pittsburgh believe that these owners have not tried very hard to put a winning team on the field. Instead, the argument goes, they have relied on the lemmings who continue to come to a beautiful ballpark built largely with public money, plus revenue sharing from the league, to take home a handsome profit. Although I don't agree with these people, I understand where they are coming from. A sports team is not like most other businesses. It is, inherently, an asset the community feels it owns. In some ways, I wouldn't mind if the community really did own the team. Then we could yell at the mayor or the governor or somebody and we could have a referendum on whether to fire the manager or sign free agents. Or maybe a bond issue for a shortstop.

But it doesn't work that way. The Pirates have been up against it, up against teams with far greater resources, no matter how hard they tried to win. They never were going to be stronger so they needed to be smarter. For eighteen years, they weren't.

****

They tried several different general managers. Ted Simmons, an eight-time All-Star catcher for the Cardinals and the Brewers, had a brief stint in 1992 and 1993 until he was forced to step aside after suffering a heart attack at the age of forty-three. Simmons was replaced by Cam Bonifay, who presided over losing seasons from June 1993 to June 2001. Bonifay was followed by David Littlefield, who continued the losing streak through 2007.

Mention some of their moves to the average Pirate fan and the response will range from a sad and knowing smile to uncontrollable rage. There were some good moves too but not nearly enough. One thing that stands out is that, after Barry Bonds left, the Pirates never had one great player. Some very good ones—Brian Giles, Jason Bay, some would say Jason Kendall—but no great ones. And not a single pitcher of note, despite spending countless first round draft picks in a quest to find one that lasted the better part of a decade.

As it happened, many of these pitchers had names that began with the letter B. They became known as the Killer Bs, as in the pitchers who almost killed the franchise. Kris Benson, first pick in the 1996 draft. Bobby Bradley, eighth pick in the 1999 draft. Sean Burnett, nineteenth pick in the 2000 draft. John Van Benschoten, eighth pick in the 2001 draft. Brian Bullington, first pick in the 2002 draft. Plus Clint Johnston, fifteenth pick in the 1998 draft. Six high first-round picks, two of them the first pick in the whole country. Together—all six of them—only fifty-two career wins in Pittsburgh.

With the eighth pick in 2003, the Pirates finally drafted a solid pitcher, Paul Maholm, who won more games for the Pirates than all of these other pitchers put together. In 2004 and 2005, the Bucs got smarter and drafted position players, Neil Walker and Andrew McCutchen, about whom much more later. But in 2006 they went back to pitching, passing up two future Cy Young winners, Tim Lincecum and Clayton

Kershaw, to select an alarmingly overused college pitcher, Brad Lincoln, who promptly needed arm surgery.

By the time the Littlefield era ended in 2007, the minor league system was a shambles. With the fourth pick in the June 2007 player draft, the Pirates passed on drafting Georgia Tech catcher Matt Weiters. Weiters was projected as a sure star, and he would become an All-Star by 2011 for the Orioles, but he was represented by an agent, Scott Boras, known for his outlandish salary demands. Instead, the Pirates chose a left-handed relief pitcher from Clemson named Danny Moskos who as of the end of 2010 was still in Double A. It turned out that Weiters was willing to sign for $6 million, far less than Boras had demanded, just as the Pirates were incomprehensibly lavishing over $13 million on washed-up pitcher Matt Morris who was summarily released less than a year later.

In late 2007 the Pirates decided to blow it all up and start over. Of the players on the Pirates' major league roster when the new general manager Neal Huntington and his boss, new club President Frank Coonelly, were hired at the end of the 2007 season, only a handful remained at the start of the 2010 season.

When Frank Coonelly and Neal Huntington came to town with the latest new plan, many people had long since tuned out. Some people were at least willing to listen. For my own reasons, I was one of them.

CHAPTER FIVE

EDEN ON THE ALLEGHENY

Pittsburgh built nearly a billion dollars in new stadiums and arenas in the first decade of the 21st century. Some of them made more sense than others. But if ever there was a case for a new stadium, it was PNC Park. Even as it has provided only misery on the field, the new stadium has been a substantial contributor to a surprisingly vibrant and resilient downtown Pittsburgh. There also is something to be said for doing a job right. People feel better about their city because of it. Painted against the Allegheny River and the Pittsburgh skyline, PNC Park is a spectacular ballpark, known and admired all over the country as perhaps the best of the new generation of baseball stadiums.

Most important, there is little question that without the new stadium, the Pirates, a Pittsburgh institution for more than a hundred years, would have been gone.

The new stadium honors that tradition. Like Three Rivers Stadium before it, and a hundred years earlier, Exposition Park, site of the first World Series, in 1903, PNC Park was built on the North Side of Pittsburgh, across the river from downtown. Someone—I wish I knew who—had a stroke of genius, that the bridge next to the stadium would be closed to cars on game days so that people could walk over the bridge from downtown. It is, as it should be, the Roberto Clemente Bridge. When you cross it, the first thing you see is a statue of Clemente and then a statue of Willie Stargell. Around the corner at home plate is a statue of Honus Wagner, star of the 1909 World Series, one of the original five inductees in the Baseball Hall of Fame and by acclamation the greatest shortstop who ever lived.

Recently, they have added one more statue, by the river, of Bill Mazeroski rounding the bases against the Yankees in 1960. Together, these statues account for every Pirate World Championship team except 1925, a matter that could be remedied by a statue of a moment that rivals Mazeroski's but which is largely forgotten, even in Pittsburgh: Kiki Cuyler's double into the dark and rainy late afternoon haze at Forbes Field as the Pirates came back with three in the bottom of the eighth against the Big Train, the incomparable Walter Johnson, to beat the Washington Senators 9-7 in the seventh game of the 1925 World Series.

In the summer of 2009, our firm moved into a new building that was being constructed farther downtown, not far from the river and the Clemente Bridge. When we chose our offices in the new building, I had only one request. I asked for one with a view of the ballpark.

As a friend who also has a view pointed out, around three o'clock on game days, players just start to appear on the field, like in *Field of Dreams*. At about 5 or 5:30, the people start to walk over the Clemente Bridge. The first time I saw them, and every time since, I have had the same reaction.

I want to go with them.

CHAPTER SIX

HOPE

Another important thing happened in the summer of 2009. The Pirates finally got a player. Credit where it is due, he was drafted out of high school in Florida in the David Littlefield era. I pretend to no special expertise but it did not take a genius to spot Andrew McCutchen. The first time I saw him I told Andee that there was only one question: star or superstar?

Andrew McCutchen is only 5'10" and about 175 pounds. But he has two rare gifts. The first is foot speed. Watching Andrew McCutchen run out a triple is a religious experience, like watching Tony Dorsett turn the corner against Georgia in the Sugar Bowl and Carl Lewis run the anchor leg of the 400-meter relay at the Los Angeles Olympics.

Andrew McCutchen's other gift is bat speed. It does not matter how big you are if you can swing the bat like that, and, as anyone who saw Michael Jordan try to play baseball knows, it does not matter how great an athlete you are if you can't.

As good as McCutchen was from the start—and he was very good—it was easy to see that he was going to be even better.

He would just need time. I would add another point, but first with an important qualifier. I don't know these players or what they are really like. I have dealt with enough athletes over the years in one context or another not to idealize any of them. Since many of them are now less than half my age, and close to the age of my children, I tend to cut them some slack as they are a lot earlier making their way through life than their fans—or even they—appreciate.

On the field, and from the very start, there was a sense of purpose about Andrew McCutchen. More than anything, the Pirates' greatest need has been to change a culture of losing, losing at historic levels, losing that has worn out player after player who has left this town beaten down and burned out, only to be reborn in another city with another team.

When I saw Andrew McCutchen I thought he could be the guy who could change that culture. Change like that doesn't happen very often. As Syd Thrift once said, "it ain't easy raising the dead." But when it happens it's a beautiful thing.

CHAPTER SEVEN

SECTION 22

As a child growing up in New York and New Jersey in the 1930s, my father saw Babe Ruth and Lou Gehrig play baseball. And Mel Ott. And Jimmy Foxx. And Lefty Gomez. In late May of 1956, after starting college, going to war—including three weeks in the hedge rows of Normandy at age nineteen—finishing college, work, marriage and a couple kids—my brother and sister—my dad would rush home to watch Dale Long as he hit home runs for the Pirates in eight straight games. I was born March 6, 1957.

My father by then had become and he remains a rabid Pirate fan. He taught me how to play baseball when I was four years old and we have watched games together for more than fifty years. I have no doubt that my lifelong love of sports has a deep connection to his. It is a very important connection.

My father is not the only baseball fan among the elders of our family. There are many others, most notably my Uncle Stanley, my mother's first cousin, actually, who was my father's fraternity brother at the University of Pennsylvania in the late 1940s, well before my father moved to Pittsburgh and met my mother. This is the kind of baseball fan my Uncle Stanley is. A couple of years ago, I read that an old

Pirate named Gus Suhr had died. I asked Uncle Stanley if he was a good player: “Well, he had a good year in ’38, but after that…”

In 2009, I went to a Pirate game with my Uncle Stanley, his son-in-law Marc, and his grandson Andrew. We were passing the time, which was all you could do with that team. Marc said that he had read that hitting five home runs in a major league game was more unusual than a perfect game. I told him that was true because it had never happened.

In the old days, men pulled guns and knives. Now they pull blackberries and iPhones. Andrew had the iPhone and he was faster on the draw. He reported that Stan Musial had hit five home runs in a game. I told him I thought it was a doubleheader. As I waited for my stodgy old blackberry to prove my point, my Uncle Stanley looked over to ask what all the yapping was about. We told him the question. He answered it in the most decisive way: "It was a doubleheader. It was in 1954, in May I think, in St. Louis.

“I was there.”

As the decades came and went, his friends got old, the Pirates got worse and my uncle got disgusted. He still went to a few games with Marc and Andrew, three generations of Pirate fans who really knew the game. At some point Marc became the keeper of the flame and purchaser of season tickets.

Years of abject failure continued; interest waned. Through Marc's good efforts, the tickets survived. A ticket group was formed. Shortly after we moved into our new office in 2009, he invited me to a game. Section 22, third base line, four rows behind the dugout.

In 2010, inspired by the new offices, Andee and I joined Marc's ticket group for ten games.

CHAPTER EIGHT

PEDRO

Most of those ten games were abysmal. As badly as the Pirates hit, they often pitched worse.

There was, however, one magical moment. I did not see it, for good reason. Our daughter Lauren was getting married the next day and we were at the rehearsal dinner on Mt. Washington, across the river and high above PNC Park. When the dinner ended, our younger daughter Rachel and her boyfriend and our son David and his girlfriend made it down the hill, across the river and into Section 22 just in time to see Pedro Alvarez bomb one into the right field seats to turn a 7-5 loss into an electrifying 8-7, 10-inning victory over the Colorado Rockies.

It was a moment to dream on, the moment of the season. Pedro Alvarez had been the second pick in the 2008 draft but many people thought he was the best player. He was second in part because his agent was the dreaded Scott Boras, scourge of small market teams. This time, though, the Pirates took Alvarez and they signed him, at the very last minute, or perhaps a moment after the deadline, as Boras briefly argued without success.

Like Andrew McCutchen, Pedro Alvarez had a chance to be a great player. Or at least a great hitter, more specifically a great power hitter, the middle of the line-up slugger the Pirates urgently needed. There were questions too, lots of them. Would he hit for average? Would he strike out too much? Could he play third base or would he have to play first? And one question especially near and dear to my heart: would he get too fat?

All good questions, but they paled next to a point by my friend Jim, a true baseball guy, who worked for the Columbus Clippers when they were a Pirate farm team in the late 1970s before he jumped the fence and went to law school. Jim is a traditionalist whom I call "old John McGraw" and who, as they say, has forgotten more baseball than I will ever know. Jim told me that when the ball comes off Pedro Alvarez's bat, it just sounds different.

CHAPTER NINE

THE DEAD SEA SCROLLS

There was one other magic moment in 2010. It was a reminder of what baseball had once meant to Pittsburgh and what it could mean again.

Over the winter, the Pirates had gone about their annual task of shopping for bargain basement free agents and various other scrap-heap signings in the hopes of uncovering a hidden gem. They rarely did, but what was the harm really? Occasionally they found someone, like Garrett Jones, the career minor leaguer who came up in June 2009 and proceeded to bop twenty-one homers in half a season. In 2010, the free agent haul included a thirty-year-old shortstop named Bobby Crosby who once had been the American League rookie-of-the-year but had fallen on hard times. It would be nice to say that Bobby Crosby was a find like Jones. He wasn't. Instead, he was traded at mid-season and then released. But this otherwise inconsequential signing is noted here because it led to a memorable observation on one of the surprisingly many well-done blogs, I forget which, that had sprung up to chronicle the efforts and exploits of this floating disaster of a Pirate ship. To wit, give or take:

"Who would have believed that Bing Crosby, who has been dead since 1977, would do more for the Pirates in 2010 than Bobby Crosby?"

Bing Crosby had been an owner of the Pirates beginning in the late 1940s. That much I knew from listening to "The Impossible Pirates" when I was five years old. What I did not know, what nobody knew, was that buried in a wine cellar in Bing Crosby's house was a treasure from the early days of television:

The full broadcast of the seventh game of the 1960 World Series.

It was the Dead Sea Scrolls of missing sporting event tapes of the twentieth century, and not just in Pittsburgh.

Bing Crosby had been so nervous about the seventh game that he couldn't bear to watch it. So he went to Paris and asked someone to record the game on a kinescope for him. How in the world this tape was not discovered for fifty years is beyond me. But there it was, in living black and white. It made its public debut at a special showing at the Byham Theater in Pittsburgh in November 2010 and then, with interviews from the Byham event spliced in, on the MLB Network.

The Byham event was moderated by Bob Costas, who, among his many gifts, has a deep and respectful sense of baseball history. The event was made all the more poignant by the presence of so many of the Pirate stars of that World Series who by then were in their late 70s and early 80s (but, sadly, not the conquering hero himself, Bill Mazeroski, who was briefly hospitalized with kidney stones): Vernon Law, the Deacon, Cy Young winner of 1960, looking like he still could pitch at age eighty. Elroy Face, the Baron of the Bullpen, who went 18-1 in 1959 and who, in the 1960s, built a bedroom closet in my in-laws' house in Greenfield (where they still live), at a time when players had real jobs in the off-season and needed them. Catcher Hal Smith, whose heroics in the fateful eighth were deprived of their rightful place in history by the even more dramatic events of the ninth. Shortstop Dick Groat, the National League MVP in 1960, also the player of the year in college basketball in 1952, and for thirty years the color commentator on the radio broadcasts of Pitt basketball games. Center-fielder Bill Virdon, the Quail, a central figure throughout the Series and in the seventh game, later twice a Pirate manager and, from a friend who golfed with him last year, at least as fit as Law. Bob Friend, stalwart pitcher for the Pirates for fifteen years, who did not fare well in the 1960 World Series. And Yankee second-baseman Bobby Richardson, the only losing team player ever to be named

World Series MVP and the only Yankee to show up at the Byham fifty years later.

All of these players were warmly remembered at the Byham event. But the biggest cheers were not for a player. Instead, they were for Vera Clemente, widow of Roberto, god of baseball in Pittsburgh, who had a hit in every game of the 1960 World Series, just as he would in another World Series eleven years later.

****

Where to begin? Forbes Field just as I remembered it, with all of its angles and distances etched in my mind more than forty years after it's been gone. 365 and the giant scoreboard with the Longines clock on top in left, the 406 mark in left center, 457 in deep left center, so deep they left the batting cage on the field during the game, the 436 mark in right center to 375 and 300 down the line, guarded by the high screen over the lower part of the covered right field bleachers. The bullpen cut into the right field corner, where Roberto Clemente would disappear and the next thing you would see would be a laser to cut down a runner at third base, if one had the temerity to try. The newsreel cameramen on the roof, just above the little third deck you could only reach by catwalk, one of whom almost went straight off the roof and onto Sennott Street chasing a foul ball that afternoon.

The straw hats that said "Beat 'em Bucs!"

The mound, much higher than today, made the 6-3 Law look eight feet tall as he gutted it out for six innings on a bad ankle. Even injured, Pirate manager Danny Murtaugh knew that Law would get the ball. On the other side, Casey Stengel was warming up relief pitchers before starter Bob Turley had even thrown a pitch. As great as they were, the Yankees had a big problem: they only had one first line pitcher, Whitey Ford, the Chairman of the Board, and he had pitched his second shutout of the Series the day before. The Bucs jumped out to a 4-0 lead with two in the first on a Rocky Nelson homer and two more in the second on a two-out hit by Virdon, until Stengel finally found a pitcher to settle things down, tiny Bobby Shantz, who took control of the game and almost ran away with it. A Moose Skowron homer in the Yankee fifth, four more runs in the sixth, including a Yogi Berra three-run homer off Elroy Face, and two more in the eighth, and it was all the way around to 7-4.

Damn Yankees.

The legendary bottom of the eighth. It began innocently enough with a bloop single by pinch-hitter Gino Cimoli.

Virdon followed with a double-play ball that's been talked about for fifty years. Well, it probably was a double-play ball, even if Virdon says it was for sure, because it was hit hard but towards the hole and Virdon could run. But then it hit something, a rock or maybe God redirected it, and it took a wicked hop and hit Kubek in the throat and everybody was safe. Groat's single to left on a barely-healed broken wrist made it 7-5, and, finally, Shantz was gone. Bob Skinner's sacrifice, when number three hitters, and everybody else, could lay down a bunt, Nelson's short fly out and the Yanks were almost in the clear. They would have been, too, if Clemente in the full flower of youth hadn't been so fast and if his chopper to first had not landed in just the right spot to freeze Yankee relief pitcher Jim Coates for the instant they needed. It was 7-6.

Then came Hal Smith, only in the game because the portly backstop, Smoky Burgess, the Little Round Man, as Bob Prince called him, had been pulled an inning earlier for a pinch runner after his second hit. As close as Hal Smith came to being a legend of American sport, he came even closer to striking out. On the 1-1 pitch, Smith took a thunderous cut, "the big ripple, the Sunday punch," as the wonderful Chuck Thompson described it on the radio broadcast that I had first heard on "The Impossible Pirates" record of my childhood. On the 1-2 pitch, any version of it in the past thirty years, Hal

Smith struck out. In 1960 it was a check swing. The Yankees barely argued. So Hal Smith didn't strike out and he lived to fight another day. On the next pitch he hit one 420 feet into Schenley Park to make it 9-7 Bucs and Forbes Field became, as Chuck Thompson described on the "Impossible Pirates," "an outdoor insane asylum."

On to the ninth. The Yankees, embodiment of Dracula then and now, would not die. A bloop by Bobby Richardson. A solid shot to right by Dale Long, Pirate hero of 1956. A rifle throw from Clemente that went off the television screen on the way to third where, I can only assume, it bore a hole in third baseman Don Hoak and continued on out of Forbes Field across Sennott Street and into the old Schenley Hotel. A pop-out by the American League MVP of 1960, Roger Maris, who was on the precipice of even bigger things in 1961, when, with [no] apologies to the inflated McGwire and Sosa, the late-day inflated Bonds and any other cartoon characters I may have omitted, he set the true single season home run record and probably shortened his life to do it. Another shot to right center by Mantle to make it 9-8 with, I cannot tell a lie, a bobble by Clemente that might have helped the tying run get to third. Gil McDougald is sent in to pinch run for Long at third but, inexplicably, as my friend Jim pointed out, only on the second pitch.

Then, the play that you have to see to believe. A hard grounder to first by Berra, Nelson tags the bag, Mantle freezes and dives back to first, which is now open, snakes around Nelson's desperate tag, McDougald scores and it's 9-9. As a close friend wrote from New York the day after the Byham show was broadcast, "I finally understand the Mantle play."

At the Byham event, there was a great interview by Bob Costas with Bobby Richardson and Dick Groat about the top of the ninth and the Mantle play. About whether Mantle screwed up and got lucky, that he should have gotten in a rundown, even if you had to be a Mickey Mantle kind of athlete to pull it off. Bill Virdon suggested that Mantle may have thought Nelson caught Berra's drive on the fly. Either way, it was an incredible play and if Mantle had not made it, the game, and the 1960 World Series, would have been over.

Bob Costas elegantly set the scene for the bottom of the ninth. Then they cut to Bill Mazeroski at the plate. We have seen it, literally, a thousand times, from behind home plate. This time we see it from center field, a shot we have never seen before, the one that shows how Maz, a high ball hitter, got a ball up on the second pitch from Ralph Terry and just crushed it.

****

There also is a DVD. It does not include the clips from the Byham event, which is a loss. But the DVD is well worth it, for many other reasons.

Especially one.

Unlike the Byham show, the DVD does not go straight to the first pitch to Maz. Instead, there is a shot of Bill Mazeroski as he settles into the batter's box. He is quietly readying himself to lead off the bottom of the ninth inning of perhaps the greatest baseball game ever played.

He is twenty-four years old. In one minute, his life is going to change forever. For me, it is the moment of moments on this tape of tapes.

I want what everyone in Pittsburgh wants, even the people who don't know it yet. One more time, just one more time, I want to see the Pirates beat the Yankees on a home run in the ninth inning of the seventh game of the World Series. In Pittsburgh.

CHAPTER TEN

THE PITTSBURGH KID

Bill Mazeroski was a local boy, from just over the Ohio border near the West Virginia panhandle. In 2004, forty-eight years after they signed Mazeroski, the Pirates drafted another local player, a high school catcher named Neil Walker from suburban Pittsburgh. Some people thought it was a grandstand play to buck up flagging interest. I didn't.

I had never seen Neil Walker play baseball but I had seen him play football for Pine-Richland High School. Walker was a big, strong kid and he was recruited by major colleges as an end. Whatever it is that makes someone an athlete, Neil Walker had it. And he had one other thing that was invaluable: both his father and his uncle had been major league baseball players. There is a wildly disproportionate number of sons and grandsons of major league players in major league baseball. We can debate why, but there is no doubt that it is true.

For all of that, Walker had languished in the farm system. Drafted in 2004, all he had to show for it through 2009 was an undistinguished September call-up. He was moved from position to position. By the beginning of the 2010 season, many considered him likely to be a wash-out. But then Aki

Iwamura, a disastrous free agent signing whom the Pirates paid over $4 million to play second base after Freddy Sanchez left, failed so quickly and completely that by the end of May the Pirates had to do something. In desperation they turned to Walker, who had barely played there.

Then Neil Walker started hitting. By the end of the year, he hit .296, with twelve home runs and sixty-six RBIs, strong numbers for any second baseman, even for a full season. He was a little big to play second base, totally untrained at the position, and the stats gurus did not like his defensive numbers much, but he was an athlete and he was a ballplayer. As far as I was concerned he wasn't half bad in the field either—and he was only going to get better.

In January 2011 we were flying to Chicago to see Lauren and her husband Nick. While waiting at the gate, Andee asked me if a young man leaning against the people mover looked familiar. I said yes, it looks like Neil Walker, because it is Neil Walker.

Nobody bothered Neil Walker that day, including us. Perhaps because the good people of Western Pennsylvania have manners. Or maybe nobody else recognized him.

They will.

CHAPTER ELEVEN

TA-BA-TA

In his golden years, my father has developed a gift for mispronunciation. He is hard of hearing, but it doesn't really matter because he watches the games with the sound off. At eighty-six, he has decided that he has listened to enough announcers for one lifetime. So, I can only assume, he sees a name on the screen or in the paper and then takes a guess, which almost invariably is wrong. This is surprising because my father, like my brother, was superb with languages, an interpreter during the war in fact, while I took four years of German to get through Dialog One.

But I would have to give my dad a pass when it comes to Jose Tabata. I have watched Jose Tabata play baseball for over a year and I do not have the slightest idea how to pronounce his name. TA-ba-ta? Ta-BA-ta? Ta-ba-TA? I have heard them all, especially the first two.

Shipped over from the Yankees with a couple other players in a second-tier trade, Jose Tabata had been viewed as a good prospect in decline, in part for supposed attitude reasons. There also may have been some uncertainty about his claimed age of twenty, fairly or not a common charge directed at Latin players, especially players like Tabata who look like they are thirty.

If Jose Tabata has any attitude issues, or any other issues for that matter, I haven't seen them. Instead, what I *have* seen since he arrived in Pittsburgh is a guy who could really play, from the day he got here. He can hit. He can run. He can field. He can throw. He plays hard, with an enthusiasm and passion this team desperately needs.

There is one baseball mystery to Jose Tabata. At 5-11, 215, he is built like a baby bull. He rockets the ball all over the field. But almost never over the wall. From time to time he will launch a monstrous shot, like the one we saw go into the right center-field bleachers, highly unusual for a right-handed hitter. But he hit only four home runs in 2010 and not many in the minors either. As the scouts say, once you have seen it, it's in there. How soon and how often, time will tell.

Even without home runs, and however his name is pronounced, in Jose Tabata, the Pirates had found another player with whom they could win. That made four, and none of them was eligible for free agency before 2016, an absolutely crucial issue for the Pirates.

McCutchen, Alvarez, Walker and Tabata. Or as they were increasingly referred to in Pittsburgh: The Future.

It had been a long time since they had one.

CHAPTER TWELVE

LEAP OF FAITH

A team needs more than four good young players. There are those who feel that a team needs to have pitching, of which the 2010 Pirates had precious little. And defense, of which they had almost none.

Whatever anyone expected of the Pirates in 2010, they were worse. The 2010 Pirates lost 105 games, the most, by far, in the entire eighteen years of losing; the most, in fact, since the epic 112-loss season of the Rinkey-Dinks of Branch Rickey in 1952.

This rock-bottom performance coincided with something of a crisis in Marc's ticket group. The problem, you will not be surprised to learn, was that nobody wanted to go. Marc didn't want to go much either but he was reluctant to give up great seats, especially when there was a family tradition to continue and at least a hint of a future. I agreed with him.

In the fall of 2010, on the heels of the worst season in fifty-eight years, I committed to go to forty Pirate games in 2011. When I told Marc, he was appreciative and cautionary. He warned me that he and Andrew had tried that one season and it was the closest to suicide he had ever come.

There were reasons. To join the people walking across the Clemente Bridge. To spend lazy summer nights at the best ballpark in the world. To watch something being built where the odds were long but not impossible. There were reasons and some of them were good reasons.

There was another reason. I had not gone to Pirate games like this in a long time. But I had done it once before.

CHAPTER THIRTEEN

1971

In the summer of 1971, I was fourteen years old. In late June, a few days before I was to leave to spend two months away at summer camp, I did one of the most idiotic things I have ever done, which is saying something. It was called chicken fighting on a bicycle. Riding at a high speed on Maynard Street, we would kick at each other. In a moment of frustration, against a kid I did not like, I threw a left hook. With that, I was over and down, with two snapped bones in my left arm and a cast to my shoulder for eight weeks.

The summer of 1971 was the hardest summer of my life. And the loneliest.

But 1971 also was the baseball summer of my childhood. The summer of Willie Stargell. Of Dock Ellis and Steve Blass. Of Bobby Robertson and Richie Hebner and Al Oliver. Of Rennie Stennett and Dave Cash. Of Vida Blue. Of Luke Walker and Bob Johnson. Of Sangy and Milt May and Charlie Sands. Of Maz and Jackie Hernandez. Of Nellie Briles and Bob Moose and Dave Guisti. Of Jose Pagan and Gene Alley. Of Gene Clines and Vic Davallilo. Of Bob Veale and Mudcat Grant and Bruce Kison.

Of Roberto Clemente.

I went to Pirate games all that summer, often by myself. Many nights, I wandered the streets of downtown Pittsburgh at midnight to catch the 61C home. It was a different time. On game days I would walk down in the morning to the old Webster Hall Hotel in Oakland to buy tickets from my new friend, an old man who worked at the ticket window there. This friendship came in handy when it came time to buy tickets for the playoff and World Series games in Pittsburgh. I went to almost all of them, the playoffs against the San Francisco Giants and the thrilling comeback in the World Series against the Baltimore Orioles, including the first night game in World Series history, when twenty-one-year-old Bruce Kison from Pasco, Washington came in and pitched six and one-third innings of game-winning relief during which he drilled three Orioles but allowed only one hit.

It has been forty years. I am fifty-four years old. How that happened, I don't know.

A better person would spend more time trying to fix this mess of a world that we are leaving our children. I know this because I am married to one.

I tell myself I am contributing in other ways. To the things that help to bind our community. To a life-affirming approach to the games we play and the importance of playing them. To the written history of our family.

The truth is I *need* to reach back. I always have. This time it came up baseball.

In the spring of 2011, the Pittsburgh Pirates went out in search of something that had been lost for a very long time.

As did I.

PART TWO

April:

CHAPTER ONE:
THE OPENER

Whatever I was looking for, I would not find it at the home opener.

Picked by just about everyone for yet another train wreck in 2011, the Pirates started out by winning two series on the road against two National League Central Division rivals—the Cubs and the Cardinals. This was no small accomplishment since the Pirates in 2010 had compiled a road record of 17-64, which only equaled the worst road record in the modern history of major league baseball.

One reason for the pre-season pessimism was that the starting pitching had been a complete disaster in 2010 and did not look much better coming into 2011. In the off-season, our Pennsylvania brothers and erstwhile bitter rivals, the large-market Philadelphia Phillies, separated now by a divisional realignment and about $125 million in payroll, had assembled a rotation of aces—Roy Halladay, Cliff Lee, Cole Hamels and Roy Oswalt—that inspired comparisons to the great pitching staffs of all time: the 1971 Baltimore Orioles, with four twenty-game winners; the Mets of Seaver, Koosman and Ryan; and, in their own city, the legendary

Philadelphia Athletics of 1929-31, featuring George Earnshaw and the immortal Lefty Grove.

As for the Pirate rotation, well, not so much. The leaders were Kevin Correia, a decent but unspectacular right hander who came over that winter from San Diego as a free agent, and Paul Maholm, the first draft choice back in 2003, a soft-tossing lefty sinker ball specialist. Neither was an ace but they both were legitimate major league pitchers.

After that, it went downhill. Ross Ohlendorf, promising when he arrived from the Yankees in 2009, went 1-11 in 2010. For this performance, and in a testament to the absurdity of modern major league baseball, Ohlendorf then was rewarded in arbitration with a substantial raise and an appalling $2 million salary for 2011.

The rest of the rotation was a couple of kids. James McDonald had come from the Dodgers at the trading deadline in 2010, in exchange for closer Octavio Dotel. McDonald, a tall, skinny right-hander with pretty good stuff, had pitched surprisingly well for the Pirates down the stretch. The question was whether he could sustain that or whether he would join the scrap heap of players like Warren Morris and Mike Brown, long-forgotten except in the dark recesses of

Pirate fandom, players who would flash promise and then quickly and permanently disappear.

Finally, there was Charlie Morton. Morton had arrived from Atlanta in mid-2009 in a trade for popular centerfielder Nate McLouth that had nearly sent the "We Hate Nutting" crowd over the edge. 2010 did not go well for Charlie Morton. Compared to Charlie Morton, Ross Ohlendorf was Sandy Koufax. By mid-season, Morton was back in the minors, possibly never to return. A big, strong kid at 6-5 and 230, Morton could throw hard and his pitches moved. There were suggestions that he was more talent than competitor, or, to be less delicate, that he lacked guts. In truth, he just seemed totally lost. The question was whether Charlie Morton ever would harness his talent.

It was not a rotation that evoked memories of the 1929 Philadelphia A's. Still, on the first road swing, the pitching had held up well enough to go 4-2. There was just enough offense, including an opening day grand slam by Walker about which one of the local writers made me laugh and want to cry by reporting that this was the first Pirate opening day grand slam since the one hit in 1962 by a player he felt the need to identify as the "Hall of Fame right fielder" Roberto Clemente.

The other noticeable change was some honest to goodness aggressive baseball. Hopefully, this was a reflection of the new manager, Clint Hurdle. The highlight was a come-from-behind Sunday afternoon win against the Cubs and closer Carlos Marmol, against whom a day earlier the Pirates had looked like they would not score in a thousand years. But this time they got a couple guys on and moving and somehow plated them on a two-run infield single by Alvarez, with Walker barreling around third to score the winning run.

****

All in all, it was pretty darn exciting. When the Bucs came home for the opener against the Colorado Rockies, a full house of over 39,000 was there to greet them with an air of expectation rarely seen at PNC Park. Even the weather gods cooperated, providing an absolutely perfect April day.

The home opener was the first of my forty games. Andee would be there too, as she would be there for the last game and as many games as she could get to in between. When something was important to me, and she knew this was, I knew that Andee would be there with me.

I often ask myself what I did to deserve a wife like Andee. I have no idea. Sometimes, I don't think Andee does either. But there is a little more to the story. Following teams and going to games is what we do as a family, what we always have done. What we still do even when our children are scattered around the country and sometimes around the world. Being together is what Andee cares about and what I care about, too.

The home opener. Andee and me, along with Marc and another close friend, Steve, whom I have known since I was six years old. We were ready to get this show on the road.

Needless to say, the Pirates were awful, from Paul Maholm's very first pitch, which was rocketed into center field. Walker then proceeded to fire a double-play ball into left field. By the time Tabata got there, late it seemed, one run was in and another was at third. Tabata and Walker redeemed themselves with hits in the first, but they were the only hits the Pirates would get until the seventh, at which point the score was 7-1, where, thankfully, it ended. It was Opening Day in Pittsburgh and the team that never missed an opportunity to miss an opportunity had missed yet another one.

CHAPTER TWO:

THE ADVENTURES OF RONNY CEDEÑO

Baseball is nothing if not symmetrical. Thanks to an invitation from my friend Jim, I was treated to an interesting if frustrating Sunday afternoon. Down 4-0 in the first, the Pirates rallied to go up 5-4. But, with the Rockies on the ropes, the Pirates couldn't finish them off. Then a rookie relief pitcher walked in the winning run, the Bucs went quietly in the seventh, eighth and ninth, and that was that.

A week later, the Pirates won almost exactly the same game in Cincinnati. This seemed to annoy the Reds, as losses to the Pirates often do. Up 4-0 in the first inning this time, the Bucs gave away the whole lead and then some, falling behind 5-4, only to rally to win on a clutch hit by Andrew McCutchen.

The Reds game also featured the next installment of The Adventures of Ronny Cedeño, the maddening Pirates shortstop. For most of the first decade of the century, shortstop at PNC Park had been manned by Jack Wilson, a very sound and occasionally brilliant defender. Wilson was dispatched to Seattle in July 2009 as part of the purge when the new management team came in, at the same time his boyhood friend and double-play partner, Freddy Sanchez, was shipped off to San Francisco.

Wilson and Sanchez were a superb double-play combination and the best part of a surprisingly excellent defensive infield on an awful team in 2009. Sanchez was known as "Boom Boom" but only to us, mostly in honor of 60s pop star Freddy "Boom Boom" Cannon, but also because he was a legitimate hitter and, in fact, a former National League batting champion. Sanchez was all the more admirable for having overcome a club foot, as had 1959 World Series hero Larry Sherry, who, along with his brother Norm and Sandy Koufax, formed the greatest group of Jewish players on any team since the Macabees, a matter of no small import to me.

Wilson and Sanchez wanted to stay together and were willing to do so in Pittsburgh, but only for a lot of money. The problem was they were reaching their early thirties and the Pirates had long since shown they were capable of losing just as well with them as without. The Pirates made Sanchez and Wilson an offer and when it was not enough, they moved them. One of the players they got in return was Ronny Cedeño.

It would be an overstatement to say that there was greatness in Ronny Cedeño. There wasn't. But he did have the raw materials, both at bat and in the field, to be a legitimate, middle of the pack major league shortstop. After he had driven the Cubs and Mariners sufficiently crazy, the Pirates were the third team to try and bring that out of him.

The problem with Ronny Cedeño was that the only consistent thing about him was his lapses in concentration. In an infield with a screaming need for stability, Cedeño could be counted on to boot well more than his share of routine grounders. Nor was he any more reliable at the plate or on the bases. He could, however, make the occasional amazing play.

All of which was on display that April Sunday in Cincinnati. With the ponderous catcher, Chris Snyder, acquired from Arizona in late 2010, on second and Cedeño on first, McCutchen fought off a two-strike, two-out pitch and knocked it into short left center. This was an excellent bit of hitting that would salvage what would have been a very tough loss. But not until Cedeño inexplicably rounded second and stormed toward third, where he slid in a millisecond, if at all, ahead of a tag that would have ended the inning well before the lumbering Snyder crossed the plate with the winning run. As we watched out of the corner of our eyes during a visit with some family, my son David and I gave each other one of those "What the ____ was that" looks that come from a lifetime of watching games together.

Then, having almost cost them the game, Cedeño proceeded to save it with a stunning stab of a liner up the middle which he turned into a double play. That is the way it goes with Ronny Cedeño and the way it will continue to go until he figures things out, as to which the clock most assuredly is running. In his way he is trying—and you never know.

Anyway, it was a win and there were three of them that weekend in the Queen City, a third straight winning road series for a team that had won seventeen road games in 2010. This at least somewhat balanced out sweeps at home to the Brewers and on the road in Florida. The NL Central was muddling along and the Pirates were muddling right with them.

The other thing muddling along was the weather. In late April, the Bucs returned home to an all-day storm that rained us out for the second time in three games. It was not all bad. It gave the Pirates a day off they could use. And it gave me a moment to drift back, something I can do better than almost anyone.

CHAPTER THREE:
HITTERS

The Pirates were not planning to muddle through the 1971 season. The Bucs were coming off their best season in a decade. In 1970, they had won the National League East, inspired I'm sure, by the catchy slogan "Go Like '60 in '70."

1970 also marked the end of Forbes Field, a double-header win over the Cubs on June 28, an inspiring afternoon and my last day of watching baseball from behind a pole, of which, for all its charm, Forbes Field had dozens. This was followed by the opening of Three Rivers Stadium, a 3-2 loss to the Reds on July 16, 1970, a game we pulled in from 300 miles away at summer camp over the 50,000 watt blowtorch, KDKA radio, which had broadcast the Pirate games forever.

The new stadium was bright and fresh, but even that could not hide the fact that its overwhelming features were that it was encased in concrete and that it was fully enclosed. In the early days, the ambiance was heightened by Germanic-themed concession stands, featuring something called a "Zum Zum Dog Mit Kraut" which seemed a bit breezy only twenty-five years after World War II.

The Bucs did not quite "Go Like '60 in '70." They came up short in the 1970 playoffs against the Big Red Machine. Still, the Pirates clearly were putting together a very good team for 1971. The strength of that team would be hitting.

The first baseman was twenty-six-year-old Bob Robertson, the "Mt. Savage Strong Boy" from rural western Maryland. Robertson was a decent first baseman, although a much better fielder, Al Oliver, had been moved to center field to get Robertson's bat in the line-up. With Popeye arms, straight out of Ted Kluszewski, Robertson could hit it a mile. He hit twenty-seven homers in 1970 and twenty-six in 1971, including one memorable shot off the face of the fifth deck in left one night against the Padres. Then he hit four home runs against the Giants in the playoffs and two more against the Orioles in the World Series.

At second base, the Pirates had an embarrassment of riches. The starter was Dave Cash, later a three-time All-Star with the Phillies. By the age of twenty-three, Cash was good enough to put an aging Bill Mazeroski on the bench. Then, in the summer, the Pirates called up another future star, twenty year-old Rennie Stennett, and all he did was bat .353.

Shortstop was the one position the 1971 Pirates devoted strictly to defense. There were two classic good-field, no-hit shortstops, each thirty years old. For much of the season, Gene Alley was the starter, as he had been for years, including in 1966, when he and Maz set a record for turning double plays. Before the 1971 season, the Pirates had acquired another shortstop, Jackie Hernandez, from Kansas City. It was a transaction of little note, then, and for most of the season. It would not end that way. Earl Weaver said the Pirates could not win a World Series with Jackie Hernandez at shortstop. Seven error-free games later, Jackie Hernandez proved him wrong.

At third base was the gravedigger, Richie Hebner, the twenty-three-year-old son of an undertaker in Massachusetts. Hebner had been the Pirates' number one draft choice in 1966 and by 1971 he already was starting his third full season in the majors. Richie Hebner was a fan favorite, especially with the young girls, for his youthful swagger, working class roots and Boston accent—all of which were featured in a classic commercial instantly known to Pittsburghers of a certain age ("It's not the bread… It's the 'wapper.'") As a third baseman, Hebner had a great arm, even if he did not always know where it was going. It was not clear that he particularly cared. Like the other young Pirates who were coming of age in 1971, Richie Hebner came to hit.

The catcher was another young hitter, twenty-seven-year-old Manny Sanguillen, the Happy Panamanian, who batted .319. There were two things that kept Sanguillen from being viewed as the best young catcher in baseball. One was Johnny Bench. The other was that he did not hit with power. What Manny Sanguillen did, better than anyone I have ever seen, and what drove pitchers crazy, was hit bad balls. Over his head. At his shoelaces. A foot outside. It didn't matter. Sangy would just keep smiling and clubbing away.

That was the infield. In the outfield, the Pirates only had two Hall of Famers and a guy who had 2743 hits. Let's start with him, since he never has quite gotten his due. Al Oliver hit .300 eleven times and made seven All-Star teams. He would have been one of the best defensive first basemen ever had he not been moved to center field to make room for Robertson. He was a good center fielder, if not quite a great one, and maybe the frustration about the unfairness of it all explained his wife's famous quote, a few years later and perhaps apocryphal, that Oliver would have been better in center if he didn't have to cover half of left. For a player who will remain unidentified here, except to say he was not the Pirate left fielder of 1971, about whom neither Al Oliver nor his wife ever would have said such a thing, even if it were true.

The right fielder was Roberto Clemente. At the age of thirty-seven, Clemente hit .341 in 1971. The things I saw Roberto Clemente do on a baseball field in 1971 are a big reason for this book. His performance in the 1971 World Series remains, I would submit, the greatest all-around performance that any player has ever put on in a World Series. For all of that, the 1971 regular season was not the season of Roberto Clemente. It was the season of the Pirates' left fielder.

It was the season of Willie Stargell.

CHAPTER FOUR:

WILLIE THE STARGE

By the end, he had more nicknames, good ones, than just about anyone who ever played. Captain Willie. Pops. Chicken on the Hill with Will. The Big Man. Willie the Starge. Even his given name, Wilver Dornel Stargell, was a nickname in the hands of Bob Prince.

There is a history to every one of them. Captain Willie was from 1979. After Clemente died, Stargell was the captain and the unquestioned leader. You have not lived until you have heard a cabin full of your twelve-year-old campers chant in rhythm and bang on anything they could find, on every important at-bat over an entire summer: "Cap-tain!...Wil-lie!" "Cap-tain!...Wil-lie!"

Pops was from then too, and later, an image the increasingly rotund grand old man would embellish with a rocking chair in the clubhouse. The Big Man was not commonly used but stuck with me from a *Sports Illustrated* article from 1970 entitled "The Big Man is the Cool Man."

Chicken on the Hill with Will is a lasting image of Pittsburgh in the 1960s. The Hill District, along with Homewood, long has been central to the black community here. For a variety of reasons, the Hill District today is a far less populous place than it was in the 1960s. Then it was booming, if not thriving. In the midst of this era, Willie Stargell and Steeler defensive back Brady Keys each opened fried-chicken restaurants on the Hill. Customers fortunate enough to be in Willie's restaurant when Stargell hit one out, which he did 475 times, would get their chicken free.

From there it was pure Bob Prince. Prince had an unmatched ability to tap into the child in all of us. When Stargell came to the plate in a key situation, Prince would implore all of Western Pennsylvania to "Think Chicken!" If he came through, Prince would scream "You can have some Chicken on the Hill with Will!" That it still gives me chills says something about me.

Before there was Chicken on the Hill there was Willie the Starge, also courtesy of Bob Prince. That one goes all the way back to when Stargell arrived in Pittsburgh in late 1962 at the age of twenty-one. Well, we thought it was at the age of twenty-one. Willie Stargell died, hauntingly, on the eve of the opening of PNC Park in 2001, just before they were to dedicate a giant statue of him outside the gate in left field. Upon his death, we learned that Stargell had not been born in 1941 as had been reported his entire baseball life, but instead in 1940. It turns out that Latin American kids are not the only ones who play around with their age.

Stargell was, however, correctly shown as having been born on March 6, same as me. I don't have to tell you that was a very big deal to a little kid in Pittsburgh, especially this one.

****

The statue of Willie Stargell at PNC Park is about twelve feet high. It is remarkably accurate except that it seems smaller than Stargell looked at the plate. He would come up and twirl his bat in giant intimidating circles. If there ever was a time when Willie Stargell tried to do anything but hit the ball into orbit, I don't remember it. If there was ever a time when I didn't think he was going to do it, I don't remember that either.

Watching Willie Stargell strike out was more exciting than watching almost anyone else hit. When he swung and missed, which he did all the time, it would take the air out of the whole stadium and there would be a huge, collective gasp. When he hit one you knew it, and when he really hit one you remembered it forever. Like the one I saw him hit over the eighty-six-foot-high right field roof at Forbes Field, which only happened eighteen times. The first was hit by Babe Ruth, his last home run, one of three the broken-down forty-year-old Ruth hit on a gray day in May 1935, and seven of them were hit by Willie Stargell.

I am too young to remember Ralph Kiner. In my lifetime, nobody in Pittsburgh ever bombed them like Willie Stargell. And Willie Stargell never bombed them like he did in April 1971. In twenty-two games, Stargell hit eleven home runs, then a record for the month of April. The one I remember most was a towering shot that bounced out an exit in the upper deck at Veterans Stadium in Philadelphia.

I watched that game in the spacious den at the home of my neighbor and summer camp friend Billy, which I often did, sometimes while he and his family were eating their meals, as his sister recently reminded me. I was, truth be told, quite an annoying little kid.

I also remember listening to Bob Prince's call of another Stargell homer in San Francisco, which I have believed for forty years happened in April but which I now have learned was in early May. I was playing pool after school and listening to the Bucs on the West Coast in the attic of a friend. The problem, I came to learn, was that my friend was starting to be more interested in other things. Or maybe it was that he didn't want to be bothered by me showing up at his house uninvited every day after school. Not that I blame him. I guess if you are going to look back, you have to look at all of it. There are many apologies owing and we can add this one to the list.

But it sure was fun playing pool and listening to Willie Stargell blast one out of Candlestick Park.

CHAPTER FIVE:

DUES

The Great Pirate Saga of 2011 began in earnest on Easter Sunday against the Washington Nationals, the first of four games in five days for me. It was not pretty. There would be no resurrection of the Pittsburgh Pirates in April 2011.

The highlight of the 6-3 loss to the Nats on Easter Sunday was that I was joined at the game by our daughter Rachel, who always makes everything better. We marked the occasion by each falling asleep in the eighth inning of an unseasonably hot afternoon where it was clear that the Pirates were going to lose. Especially after two of the Nationals' fifteen hits left the ballpark. The second of which—by former Pirate Adam LaRoche, who never hit when he was in Pittsburgh until after the season was irretrievably lost, which in fairness to Adam usually was pretty early—was decidedly of the salt in the wound variety, as the faithful around us made clear to LaRoche as he circled the bases.

The big story of game number two was the attendance. It was a make-up game on a cold and rainy April night when the Penguins were playing across the river in the Stanley Cup playoffs. An Orange County, California blogger posted a series of pictures counting the house section by section, allowed for a percentage of fans in the rest rooms and concession lines, and came up with an estimated attendance of 1100. I felt this was grossly unfair. I counted almost 1500.

The game itself was quite good, featuring a strong pitching performance by Paul Maholm. Maholm quickly gave up two runs in the first and then shut down the Nats on one more hit through the seventh. After a rain delay, the Pirates took the lead on a two-run double by someone named Brandon Wood, who had been scooped up off the waiver wire to light a fire under Cedeño at short and back up Alvarez at third. It also featured something else I did not see in any of the other three games I attended that week or during the rest of April.

A win.

The third game was terrific too, featuring the new and improved Charlie Morton battling pitch for pitch with Giants' star Matt Cain for over six innings. Morton left in a jam in the seventh ahead 2-1. But Chris Resop, a scrap heap reliever who had spent time in Japan and who had pitched very well for the Bucs, put out the fire, culminating in a thrilling eleven-pitch strike-out of Mike Fontenot. It was the kind of game where every little play mattered. Unfortunately, after Pirate reliever Evan Meek, an All-Star in 2010, lost his third lead of the month, on his way to the disabled list for most of the year, the Giants made one more play than the Pirates.

After an off night for me, a 2-0 Pirate win of course, I was back the next afternoon. A friend had something come up and I ended up crossing the Clemente Bridge alone. He didn't miss much. The Pirates only had four hits, three of them by Neil Walker, and they made four errors in losing to the Giants and former Pirate pitcher Ryan Vogelsong, who had not won a major league game in five years.

I totaled up the damage. Five days. Four games. Three losses.

****

After the Bucs split the first two with the Rockies in Denver, April was in the books. The Pirates were an almost respectable 12-15. They had pitched much better than expected, especially Correia and Morton. Except for the injured Meek, the bullpen had held up very well. The defense was a mixed bag. The old school statistics said the Pirates were among the worst defensive teams in baseball. The new-fangled ones of course said they were one of the best. To me, there was truth in both. There were plenty of jaw-dropping plays, good and bad.

The biggest problem the Pirates had was they couldn't hit. They struck out constantly, struggled to get the big hit and went down far too easily in the late innings. As I emailed to friends during the final loss to the Giants:

"Bucs need a little more never say die. Before I do."

The other problem the Pirates had, apparently, was me. I had gone to six games in April and I was 1-5. Most of the games had not been great. A couple of them were terrible. There was, however, one thing that I began to notice, even in the bad games and the losses and the constant rain. It was the thing I had been hoping for when I got myself into this.

I was starting to love baseball again.

May:

CHAPTER ONE:

A GOOD DAY FOR ALL CONCERNED

With two more road wins to start May against the Rockies and Padres, the Pirates closed to within one game of the elusive .500 mark at 14-15. New manager Clint Hurdle made clear that reaching .500 was not an important milestone to him, advice his team took to heart the following night when they blew two different two-run leads in losing to the last-place Padres. Still, when the Pirates closed out the San Diego series the next day with another win, they had won more road series than they had in all of 2010. Even more surprising, for the moment, they had the best road record in baseball.

The series-clinching win in San Diego was highlighted by a grand slam by catcher Ryan Doumit. Doumit was one of the last holdovers from the prior regime. He had struggled as a defensive catcher from the beginning. In one of his earliest games, David and I had watched in amazement as Doumit threw down to third after strikeouts and the third baseman had to leap to catch it. Finally, he threw one into left field, something I have never seen before or since. Doumit also had been beset by injuries. But he was a major league hitter, at least when he batted left-handed as he usually did, and there were times when he was a very good major league hitter.

As Doumit's injuries mounted and his defense deteriorated even more, the Pirates felt the need in late 2010 to acquire another veteran catcher from Arizona, the hulking Chris Snyder. Snyder was a significant upgrade on defense. If he was not quite the all-around hitter Doumit was, he could hit with power from time to time.

The Snyder trade did not make Doumit happy, of course. Doumit also appeared disheartened to have been left behind in Pittsburgh when the players he came up with were almost all gone and the team was a disaster. Freddy Sanchez was on his way to winning a World Series, Jason Bay had played in one and Ryan Doumit was stuck in Pittsburgh on a team that lost 105 games.

By the end of 2010, it was pretty clear that Ryan Doumit had come to view his time with the Pirates as a hostage situation. It was a very close race as to who wanted most to see Ryan Doumit leave Pittsburgh—the Pirates, Doumit or me. They had tried to trade Doumit over the winter, without success. The problem was that, after a particularly promising stretch, the Pirates had rewarded Doumit with a five million dollar a year contract. It had not been entirely irrational at the time.

In the meantime, the Pirates were left in the incongruous position of spending nearly $10 million of one of the lowest payrolls in baseball on two catchers who were ordinary at best. Doumit wanted out, the Pirates wanted to move him, and the best way for that to happen was for him to start to hit. When Ryan Doumit broke up the last game of the road trip with a grand slam, it was a good day for all concerned.

CHAPTER TWO:

FIREWORKS

After a loss that brought my record to 1-6, the Pirates bounced back in my absence behind another superb pitching performance by Charlie Morton to rout the Astros before a Fireworks Night crowd of over 32,000. People in Pittsburgh love their fireworks. Sometimes I think the Pirates would draw better if every night was Fireworks Night and they sprinkled in a handful of Baseball Nights.

Actually, the Pirates draw remarkably well. Their attendance in losing 105 games in 2010, their eighteenth losing season in a row, exceeded their attendance in the World Championship seasons of 1971 and 1979. A big part of it is PNC Park. A lot of people, and for many years I was one of them, will go out a few times a year just to spend a summer night at a beautiful ballpark.

The Pirates' ability to draw fans also is a grudging tribute to modern sports marketing, which never allows even a moment of silence at any sporting event. So now we get Fireworks Nights, pierogie races, washed-up rock stars and bobbleheads (of which I would have quite a valuable collection from the early 1960s if I had not shattered most of them and, I confess, eaten part of one, when I was six). All of this makes PNC Park a "family-friendly environment," even if it can be highly distracting to the people who actually want to watch the game.

****

The next day was Mother's Day and Rachel's birthday, so we were watching at home. James McDonald was excellent. When he left after six innings it was 2-0 Bucs and McDonald had struck out eight.

This made it all the more frustrating when the bullpen promptly gave up three runs in the seventh. The telling thing was that I was upset about it. For so many years, I really didn't care. But this time I was upset, upset at the bullpen, upset at the shoddy infield defense, upset at the umpire who called a spectacular catch by Andrew McCutchen a trap in the eighth. I even was a little upset with McCutchen for stopping to protest while Carlos Lee lumbered into second, from where he would move to third on a pick-off throw into center and score on a sacrifice fly that turned a 2-0 lead into a 4-2 deficit. This game was setting up as another tough late-inning loss.

The other telling thing was that, when Andee went into the kitchen to make dinner, for the first time in memory—maybe ever—she put the game on the kitchen radio. The radio was a half-second ahead of the television broadcast. That was why, even before I saw it, I could hear Ryan Doumit's dramatic, game-winning, right-handed, no doubt about it, three-run blast into the left field seats in the bottom of the eighth.

Earlier in the week, I had subjected a friend to a lengthy diatribe about how I could not wait until Ryan Doumit left town. To me, he was the last of the players who had been beaten down by all the losing. He had not handled it well in 2010. As I told my friend, Doumit could hit ten home runs in a week and I still would want him gone.

Since then, Ryan Doumit has hit two enormously important home runs and guided a young pitcher through a masterful outing. With the encouragement of Clint Hurdle, Ryan Doumit now is handling a difficult situation like a pro. I am starting to wonder—and I never admit this—if I might be wrong.

CHAPTER THREE:

FATHER'S DAY

For the Dodgers, it was a raw deal that may have cost them the game. For the Pirates, it was justice for the bad call they had to overcome the day before. For me, it was an early Father's Day gift to my dad. Any way you look at it, when Jose Tabata's diving effort on Juan Uribe's sinking liner was ruled a catch rather than a trap, which it apparently was, the Pirates had a double play instead of second and third, with nobody out, in the top of the eighth of a 1-1 game. Within minutes, Uribe and Dodger manager Don Mattingly had been ejected; Garrett Jones had walked; Neil Walker, Lyle Overbay and Ryan Doumit each had doubled to right; and your Pittsburgh Pirates were above .500 this late in the season for the first time since May 29, 2004.

It is an accepted fact in our family that I am not always the perfect son. Unlike my sister, who regularly calls from Boston, I can go weeks at a time without speaking to my parents, who are in their 80s and live only a mile or two away. In my defense, my parents still lead active and independent lives. My mother is a library researcher by training who, when I was about six, went back to grad school, nearly fifteen years after graduating—she would want me to be sure to include—from Smith College. For many years, she put out an index of scholarly articles on the Middle East that was used by libraries all over the world. A few years ago she wrote a book with the inspired title *For Grandmas Who Do Windows,* to teach seniors to use computers. My mother also remains an active bridge player who more than holds her own in the rough and tumble world of duplicate bridge. A Silver Life Master, I'm told, or, as my mother modestly puts it, one of the better B-group players in the area. And, on a personal and historical note, she is a great cook.

After forty years of lugging cases of shoes to the steel and coal towns of Western Pennsylvania, Eastern Ohio and West Virginia, which he loved, and then running the office, which he tolerated, my father likewise has had a model retirement. His life is so full of worthwhile activities that I use it to argue to my wife, thus far without success, that she should not be terrified by the prospect that someday I might not be at work every day. He teaches English to Russian immigrants who revere him, because he cares about them and they know it. One night, in the middle of a Pirate game at PNC Park, he rattled off seven of their phone numbers from memory. He is involved in political campaigns. He has been part of a group that recreates old-time radio broadcasts from the 1930s and 40s and he sings in a choral group, for, as he puts it, "any old folks' home who will have us."

One reason that my parents put up with me is that I am their son. Another is that, as my mother graciously allows, "we don't always count on you for the little things but we know we can count on you for the big things." One of those big things was in the summer of 2005, when my father went to the Cleveland Clinic at the age of eighty for a second opinion about his heart, was told that he was too sick to leave, then was told that it was hopeless and there was no point in operating. In a panic, we called his cardiologist in Pittsburgh, a family friend who was only about eighty-seven then and today, well into his nineties, still is helping patients, including my father. He consulted with one of his old students, a mere lad of sixty-five who became my father's cardiologist at Cleveland Clinic and guided him in the most careful and thoughtful way through a major surgery and several delicate follow-up procedures that lasted nearly a month and saved his life.

All of which makes my father's continued vitality at eighty-six the more remarkable. Having been reminded of the mortality of it all, I have tried to be more attentive. We still do what we always have done, just a little more of it. We go to Pitt football and basketball games. We have been to the NCAA Tournament. We watch games together on television. His favorite sport was tennis, which he played for seventy years, including in his youth on the municipal courts of New Jersey with a kid named Dick Savitt who was a couple years younger and who grew up to become the champion of Wimbledon. You could look it up. But now my dad only can play golf, and we play on a municipal course on Sundays in a land far, far away.

If there was to be a great Pirate saga in 2011, it was important to me that my father be part of it. This took some advance planning. There are twenty-five or thirty rows of steps that take you to Section 22, which is too many for my dad. The Pirates were very helpful in setting up an alternate route. We were in our seats long before Jeff Karstens worked confidently through sixty-four pitches over five innings and labored mightily through twenty-six more in the sixth. We were still there when Joel Hanrahan closed out the ninth on the second of two terrific plays at third by Pedro Alvarez. Every lazy fly ball by the Dodgers, and I mean every one, was a "can a corn" just like Bob Prince taught us both fifty years ago.

When the Pirates won, there were high-fives all around, not just me and my dad, but also the guy in front of us and his dad. Hope was stirring in the hearts of old men and their middle-aged sons. The Pirates were 18-17 and the reason, of all things, was pitching.

CHAPTER FOUR:

RADIO BALL

The Pirates never has been a pitchers' franchise. Twelve players elected to the Baseball Hall of Fame spent the largest portion of their careers in Pittsburgh. Clemente, Stargell and Mazeroski from the modern era. Ralph Kiner from the post-war era. Honus Wagner, player-manager Fred Clarke and Jake Beckley from the early days. Max Carey and Arky Vaughn from the 1920s and 30s, along with Paul and Lloyd Waner—Big Poison and Little Poison—of whom at least Paul was aptly named since legend has it that he was a raging alcoholic who often played, and played well, when he was stone drunk. And Harold "Pie" Traynor, star third baseman of the Pirate World Series teams of the 1920s, the 1925 World Champions and the Pirate team that was swept by the team against which all baseball teams are measured to this day, the 1927 New York Yankees.

When I was a kid, Pie Traynor was better known for the American Heating ads ("Who Can? A-mer-i-can!"), which left us comforted in the knowledge that there would be no payment due "until the roses bloom next summer." An iconic Pittsburgh commercial, most famous for Pie Traynor appearing live and in person on Studio Wrestling on Saturday nights with Chilly Billy Cardille, Pittsburgh's own

Bruno Sammartino and Ringside Rosie. But not THE iconic Pittsburgh Pirates commercial, which, for your listening pleasure, I hereby sing from memory as could any even half-serious Pirate fan of the 1960s. "Ready, Conchita:

> Joseph Ziskind takes your house out of hiding.
> Brr-rightens it up with aluminum siding.
> No money you'll be riskin' if you call Joe Ziskind
> So dial that number and do it quick.
> Hazel 1-7866.
> Hazel 1-7866."

I digress. The point is that none of these twelve Hall of Famers was a pitcher and the Pirates have never had one. There have been a few Hall of Fame pitchers who passed through here. Goose Gossage put on quite a show in the summer of 1977. The Pirates first saw that a failed starter could become a dominant reliever. Bert Blyleven pitched here for a few years in the late 1970s, including on the 1979 World Series team, with the most beautiful curveball you ever saw. Jim Bunning even stopped by for a couple years before embarking on a long career in the lunatic fringe of the United States Senate, after great years in Detroit and a perfect game for the Phillies on Father's Day in 1964, news I bolted out of the Parkway Cabana Club swimming pool to report.

None of these pitchers spent their best years in Pittsburgh. The Pirates were a hitting franchise and that was just the way it was, especially in the 1970s.

****

Pirate pitching was good enough in 1971. Good enough to win a World Series against a team that had four twenty-game winners.

In the mid-1960s, Bob Veale was the best pitcher the Pirates had. There were times when he was the only pitcher the Pirates had. A bespectacled 6-6 giant of a man from pre-integration Alabama, Veale led the National League in strikeouts in 1964, right in the middle of Sandy Koufax's six years from God. If he was not as fast as Koufax or Pittsburgh Central Catholic's own Sudden Sam McDowell, he was close. At the key moments, Bob Prince would urge Veale to give them "the radio ball," the one they could hear but couldn't see. By 1971, Bob Veale was thirty-five and in the bullpen. He only pitched forty-six innings and his ERA was 6.99. But he went 6-0 and if any Pirate deserved to pitch in the 1971 World Series, it was Bob Veale.

Nelson Briles should have been just entering his prime, but he wasn't. He didn't know it but his prime already was in the past. Briles had been a star at a young age, going 14-5 for the World Champion Cardinals in 1967, winning most of them after Roberto Clemente had put the Cards' season in jeopardy with a line drive that broke Bob Gibson's leg. Briles then won 19 games to help the Cards to another pennant in 1968. A talented guy beyond baseball, Briles excelled at doing impressions, most famously, at least in those days, of smarmy minor celebrity Paul Lynde of the *Hollywood Squares* TV show. Injuries would shorten his career and he died young, after a stint as a Pirates broadcaster. In 1971, Nellie Briles did a lot of good things for the Pirates and one great thing—a two-hit shutout, falling off the mound on nearly every pitch, in the fifth game of the 1971 World Series.

Luke Walker had been a rising star, going 15-6 when the Pirates won the National League East in 1970. He did not match that in 1971, or ever again, but he won ten games that season and he provided some magic for my dad and me on a late Sunday afternoon in July when he took a no-hitter into the ninth inning against the Dodgers. Bob Johnson came over from Kansas City, where he had struck out 206 batters. If those strikeouts did not come with him to Pittsburgh, Johnson did give them 27 starts in 1971 and then he won a playoff game against the Giants.

There was a little bit of youth sprinkled in. The best of them was Bruce Kison, a baby-faced kid who came up at mid-season. He was 6-4 and only 175 pounds and he threw side-arm. They called him The Whip. When he came up in July he brought some juice to the staff right away and, as the Orioles would find out in the World Series, that baby face belied a very competitive young pitcher.

****

You cherish a season like 1971 while you can. In 1971, the future could not have been more promising for Bob Moose from Export, Pennsylvania, just outside Pittsburgh. He was only twenty-three years old and already he was an established pitcher for his hometown team. In the majors by the age of twenty, Moose had broken through in 1969, going 14-3 and pitching a no-hitter against the Miracle Mets in Shea Stadium.

But all manner of tragedy lay ahead for Bob Moose, and soon. Bob Moose threw the wild pitch that let in the winning run in the deciding game of the 1972 playoffs against the Reds after, it is usually forgotten, almost pitching out of the two-on, nobody-out calamity to which he had entered. In 1974, he was diagnosed with a blood clot in his shoulder. He would never be the same pitcher. Then, on October 9, 1976, married and with a young daughter, Bob Moose was killed in a car crash. On his twenty-ninth birthday.

****

The heart of the 1971 Pirate staff was three pitchers who were in their prime. Dave Guisti was the finest Pirate relief pitcher since Elroy Face. After a decent but unspectacular run as a starter for the Astros through the 1960s, and a brief layover with the Cards, Guisti found his place in the Pirate bullpen. He was not a flamethrower. Instead, he relied on a tough mindset and something called a palm ball. Relief pitchers were used differently in 1971. Their roles were not as rigidly defined and closers often came in well before the ninth inning. But a good team still needed to have a good closer and the Bucs had one in Dave Guisti.

You could write a book on how Dock Ellis wasted a special talent and, in fact, Dock Ellis did. It is called *Dock Ellis in the Country of Baseball.* Appropriately, Ellis wrote this book in collaboration with a man named Donald Hall who became the poet laureate of the United States. Everything Dock Ellis did was outsized. He died young but Dock Ellis got his money's worth.

The one year Dock Ellis did not waste his talent was 1971, the year he was chosen to start the All-Star game back when the All-Star game really mattered. In 1969, we only were allowed to watch television at our summer camp two times the entire summer, to see Neil Armstrong walk on the moon and to watch the All-Star game. At the All-Star break in July 1971, Dock Ellis was 14-3, nearly as good as his opponent, rookie sensation Vida Blue, who had gone 17-3 for the Oakland A's. Like Ellis, Blue also would squander much of his career, putting the lie to the commercial he did that summer that assured a concerned nation that "success isn't gonna spoil Vida Blue."

Blue and the American League would win that 1971 All-Star Game, despite a long home run to right center by Clemente. Ellis took the loss. Whether it was Reggie Jackson's titanic home run that night off the light tower in Tiger Stadium, a tired arm or, with Dock Ellis, who knows what else, he was not the same pitcher after the All-Star game. Still, he went 19-9 and the Pirates don't get to the World Series without the kind of year Dock Ellis had in 1971.

By the time they got to the World Series, Steve Blass, not Dock Ellis, was the Pirates' best pitcher. Blass had come up with the Bucs in the mid 1960s and by 1971 he already had carved out a nice career. 1971 was one of four seasons in which Steve Blass would win fifteen games or more. In 1972 he would win nineteen and finish second in the National League's Cy Young voting. Then, out of nowhere, he just lost it. He could not throw strikes. He tried everything and nothing worked.

By the beginning of 1974, when he was only thirty-two years old, his baseball career was over. To this day, it is called Steve Blass Disease and when a pitcher gets it, like Rick Ankiel or Mark Wohlers, Steve Blass has to relive it all over again.

This he does, graciously, from his seat in the Pirate broadcast booth at PNC Park. I have lived in the same city as Steve Blass for almost fifty years and have never met him. I feel as if I know him, though, the way you know someone you have heard speak for hours and hours. The Steve Blass I think I know is a gentleman, with a keen and light sense of humor, and a perspective on the joy and sadness of life. He also is, I hope, content in the knowledge that when it is time to throw the cards on the table for what you did in this world, it won't be lending his name to Steve Blass Disease. Instead, it will be this: a 2-1, heart stopping, complete game win over Frank Robinson, Brooks Robinson and Boog Powell, all the nonsense that Earl Weaver could come up with that day, which was a lot, and the big, bad Baltimore Orioles, the self proclaimed "Best Damn Team in Baseball," in Memorial Stadium in Baltimore on a cold and gray October Sunday afternoon in the seventh game of the 1971 World Series.

CHAPTER FIVE:

FACT CHECK

In May 1971, the Pirates started to make their move. Only 12-10 at the end of April, the Bucs finished the month 29-19. Dock Ellis went 4-0 for the month, gave up only eight runs in five starts and out-dueled the young Nolan Ryan. Willie Stargell continued his assault on the National League, finishing the month with seventeen homers and forty-three RBIs, a pace he would maintain the entire season. As May turned into June, the Pirates served notice of the kind of team they were going to be, taking four straight from the Cubs and the Cardinals and outscoring them 35-1.

How do I know this, you may ask. There now is a website called baseball-reference.com. It contains detailed information on virtually every team, every player, and every play of every baseball game ever played. A person with the inclination and the time could spend his whole life on this website. If I had more time, I could be that person.

I love the past. I loved the past even before I had one. In my misspent youth, I often would wander down to Carnegie Library in Oakland, just across from Forbes Field, and page through old newspapers on microfilm to read about sports and other important events in twentieth century history.

There are times when I feel the best thing about the present is that someday it will be the past.

So I could wile away the hours on baseball-reference.com if I had the time. It reminds you of things you had forgotten. It fills in the gaps of the things you remember. It corrects little inaccuracies you have carried in your mind for decades. It is true and limited in the way that numbers are. Someday, they will make this site even better by adding a link to the newspaper stories or even the broadcasts, and then these games truly will come back to life.

Someone could write a book just reliving baseball through baseball-reference.com. But it would not be this book. In truth, I remember very little about those Pirate games of May 1971, save the Stargell homer in San Francisco that I have been certain for forty years happened in April. My summer of love with baseball did not begin until that summer, until I got hurt and all my friends were gone, and the Pittsburgh Pirates were the one thing I looked forward to every day. And I remember the most important parts very well.

CHAPTER SIX:

GROUND CHUCK

Well, that was fun while it lasted. After inching over the coveted .500 mark, the Pirates proceeded to lose six straight. The first two were at home to the Dodgers, perhaps revenge of the baseball gods for the Pirates' gift-wrapped victory in the first game of the series. It might have been three straight had the final game not been washed out after an early 1-0 Dodger lead, but only after we sat through a two-hour rain delay. That made two rain-outs, two rain delays and a game played in a driving rainstorm if you're scoring at home.

The rain-out did allow us to watch the entire no-hitter pitched by the Candy Man, John Candelaria, against the Dodgers in 1976 on the giant scoreboard video screen. This also led to a brief discussion with Marc and Andrew about how many players on this Pirate team could have started on the 1976 team. Consensus: not many.

(A few years ago, I was in a back corner of an airport, Charlotte I think. I was waiting for a connecting flight and reading *Sports Illustrated*. There was an article on tall pitchers, including John Candelaria. I looked up from reading the article and there was the Candy Man. I had not seen him in twenty years and I have not seen him since.)

After losing two to the Dodgers, the Pirates then embarked on their first 2011 visit to their own special house of horrors, Miller Park in Milwaukee. As I'm sure you have figured out by now, the statistical measures of the Pirates' eighteen years of futility can defy belief. Is it humanly possible that a team can go 33-3 at home over another major league baseball team over a five-year period? That's where it stood after another three-game sweep, led by the part-Jewish slugger Ryan Braun (the slugging Hank Greenberg part, I choose to believe, and not the part that has participated in if not precipitated a pretty active, recrimination and bean-ball-laden feud between the Pirates and Brewers over the past few years). Braun hit more homers and drove in more runs in the series than Pedro Alvarez had all season. The losing streak then reached six in Washington before it was interrupted mercifully, if not surprisingly, by yet another rain-out, albeit on a day when it did not actually rain.

All of which must have driven the division-leading Reds out of their gourds when the Bucs snapped back to take two in a row in Cincinnati. That made five out of six against the Redlegs, all on the road. Whatever else, the Pirates already were having an impact on the pennant race. This mini-sweep featured a 5-0 shutout by Charlie Morton, his second complete game victory over the Reds, highlighted by long bombs by Pedro Alvarez, a welcome sight, and Andrew

McCutchen. The media had taken to calling Morton "Ground Chuck." Morton had altered his delivery over the winter from overhand to three-quarters, a radical and courageous move at this point in his career. The result was a slight drop in velocity but a nasty, biting sinking fastball that would yield fourteen ground ball outs against the Reds to go with five strikeouts. A year earlier, Charlie Morton was in free fall. Now, for the moment, he was the stopper and the Pirates were coming home on a two-game winning streak to take on the prodigal son, Jim Leyland, and the Detroit Tigers.

CHAPTER 7:

RANT, RANT, RANT FOR THE HOME TEAM

A friend recently told me that his ninety-one-year-old mother explained to him that the secret to living a long life is to always have a long list of scores to settle. This is not a problem for the Pirates, of course, or me for that matter.

One of them is with Jim Leyland, odd as that sounds. Jim Leyland did a magnificent job managing the Pirates. All of the winning seasons the Pirates have had in the past twenty-eight years have been with Jim Leyland as manager. He always says nice things about the Pirates and, as for Pittsburgh, he still lives here for goodness sake.

Nevertheless, for me, there always will be an asterisk next to Jim Leyland's good works in Pittsburgh for 1996, when, in my view, he jumped ship in perhaps the darkest hour of the franchise. I am sure there are two sides to the story and I don't know either one of them. But if a score must be settled as Leyland and the Tigers came to town for a three-game interleague series, well, this would just have to do.

Especially after Leyland took the opportunity to say good things about the current Pirate team and the way they are being run. Not just good things, but credible things. Fortunately, Leyland also made a few comments about interleague play to get me going; specifically, that he does not like it, in part because the two leagues have different rules. Fair enough, as far as that goes, but Leyland then reportedly went on to say that interleague play penalizes the American League, which uses a designated hitter. That, along with the overarching need to find something to get mad about here, yields the following stored up baseball grievances, which I have had for a long time but only now feel that I have standing to raise:

1. The designated hitter. I am not a "time begins on opening day" rhapsodizer. When I hear people like that, I get the same chalk on the blackboard feeling I get when I listen to one of those NPR interviews where a bird tweets in the background. But, as with NPR, just because I can't stand to listen to them doesn't mean I don't agree with them. And just because the American League came up with the designated hitter gimmick in response to a dip in fan interest in the early 1970s doesn't mean that it's baseball. They could skip extra innings and have tie games decided by a round of home run derby. It would be exciting. But it wouldn't be baseball. (It would be hockey.)

2. The remaining grievances fall under the heading of disrespect, source of nearly all grievances in today's world, in this case disrespect, however well-earned and richly deserved, of the Pittsburgh Pirates. To wit:

** There are thirty teams in baseball. That fits perfectly into fifteen teams in each league and five teams in each division. Instead, there are 16 teams in the National League and fourteen teams in the American League. To win the National League Central Division, where the Pirates play, you have to beat five teams. To win the AL West, you have to beat three teams. That is ridiculous. It is especially ridiculous because the Milwaukee Brewers are the old Seattle Pilots of the AL West. So move them back to the AL West. In fact, maybe they can move back to Seattle, especially since the Pirates can't beat them in Milwaukee. For eighteen years, the Pirates have had nothing to say on this issue. It occurred to me to wait until they had a contender. But that would be sour grapes. This is only pre-sour grapes.

**As for interleague play, unlike Jim Leyland, I happen to like it. You get to see players you would never see. Like the time the gifted but troubled Albert Belle came to Pittsburgh with the Chicago White Sox. When Belle went out to play left field, near where we were sitting, he was greeted by a chorus of boos. Our son David, who had just turned nine, started to join in. I explained to him that we don't boo. A couple minutes later, a foul ball down the left field line bounced off the wall and rolled about two feet behind Albert Belle. Belle did not move an inch. A ball boy finally had to run all the way from by the dugout and circle behind Belle to get the ball. Belle still did not move. Not one inch. David looked at me and smiled: "Can we boo him now, Dad?"

Actually, we had liked Belle when he had played with the Indians a couple years earlier. I had a case in Youngstown just as the Indians were starting to get good for the first time in ages. It was the year Albert Belle hit fifty home runs. I used to eat lunch at McDonald's during breaks in the depositions. They were selling child-sized Indians helmets. I bought one for each of the kids, who were in grade school. A few weeks later, the Indians were in the playoffs. I went upstairs and all three children were at the foot of our bed, face forward in front of the TV, cheering on the Indians, with their Indians helmets on backwards on their happy little heads.

So I like seeing American League teams and I like interleague play. I would like it even more if the Pirates played home and home every year with the Indians, who are only 142 miles away. That way, the Pirates might feel more like the teams that really seem to matter, like the Yankees and Mets and the Cubs and White Sox, who do play each other every year, which is why they still have interleague play. In fact, on Saturday night the Pirate game was blacked out because of a deal major league baseball apparently struck where everybody else in baseball had to shut down their local television so that Fox could show either the Yankees and the Mets or the Cubs and the Red Sox to the whole country. Nice.

For the Pirates though, things actually worked out pretty well this one time, contributing to a sellout crowd on a rare beautiful spring night. On this night, the Pirates got the timely hit and took the extra base and the Tigers had the sloppy plays and the bad at-bats at the wrong times. Even if the Bucs were shut down and shut out the next day, missing a chance to climb back to .500, they had fought back from the six-game losing streak. It was the first point at which they could have collapsed, as they have collapsed so many times for so many years, and they didn't.

The 2011 Pittsburgh Pirates may not yet be a team to dream on but they are a team that deserves a few rants on its behalf.

CHAPTER EIGHT:

THE FANTASTIC RONNY C

The Pirates finished May at 25-28, in fourth place, six and a half games behind the division-leading Cardinals in the NL Central. The highlight of the month was a 10-0 win in Chicago that may have been the best baseball game the Pittsburgh Pirates have played in many years. It featured a brilliant performance by Paul Maholm, a ninety-one-pitch, three-hit shutout that easily could have been a perfect game. The Bucs hit four home runs that day, including a three-run opposite field homer to break open the game by Ronny Cedeño, now known to us, at least for the moment, and for reasons that shortly will be explained, as the Fantastic Ronny C.

Fittingly, May closed with a two-and-a-half hour rain delay at Wrigley Field on Memorial Day weekend. There was a saving grace. A Cubs broadcaster had put together fabulous tapes of Hall of Fame broadcasters, including Bob Prince. They played some of it during the rain delay. These audio clips included numerous calls by Prince for "Bubushka Power" which I had completely forgotten, by which he would urge the hard-working ethnic women of Western Pennsylvania of 1975 to wave their bubushkas to carry the Buccos to victory, just as Pirate fans had waved the Green Weenie on the Gunner's say-so in 1966. It was the kind of broadcasting you just don't hear anymore, including Bob Prince passing the time by saying that he often wondered whether, if they put everything he drank before he had to quit into one giant swimming pool, it would float the Queen Mary.

(The Pirates' excellent and at times outrageously funny color man, Bob Walk, gets as close to the line as you can these days. Earlier this year, play-by-play man Greg Brown was talking about the questionable readings on the radar gun, whether Aroldis Chapman of the Reds really throws 106 miles an hour and so on. Finally, Walk chimed in to say, give or take: "I agree with you. In fact I was just having a conversation about that the other day with an officer on Route 79.")

Now, back to baseball. The 25-28 record also meant that the Bucs were 13-13 in May. This was pretty darn good by Pirate standards, especially considering that they ended the month with twenty percent of the team on the disabled list, including, in addition to Ross Ohlendorf, who had been out pretty much all year, Pedro Alvarez, who added a leg injury to a month and a half of hitting .208 with two homers and—worst of all—a broken ankle to Ryan Doumit that would sideline him until August.

It took some good things and some bad things to play .500 baseball in May. The short version is that the pitching was excellent and the hitting was awful. The slightly longer version is that the starting pitching was superb, the relief pitching was adequate and closer Joel Hanrahan was dominant, closing all fourteen of his save opportunities in the first two months. Also, the defense was cleaner in May, in large part due to the Fantastic Ronny C, heretofore the source of rampant defensive instability, but who ended May with a rock solid thirty-seven-game errorless streak. And the hitting was awful.

Through two months, the Pirates had looked like something they had not looked like in a long time: a competitive major league baseball team. There were moments when a person of a mind to do so, say, for example, a person who had committed to go to forty games, could start to believe.

May also was the month when it became clear that the Pirates now had a defining personality. It was the new manager, Clint Hurdle. This guy was a pro and he had a presence that had not been seen in a Pirate dugout for many years, probably since Jim Leyland. Hurdle took charge in his dealings with the players, some public and doubtless many others behind the scenes. He took charge in his remarks to the media and in his discussions with umpires. Most of all, he took charge in two key moves that paid dividends in May. First, he benched Ronny Cedeño for arguing with an umpire instead of running out a ground ball. Then, to make clear that rules apply to everyone, even the best player on the team, he did the same thing to Andrew McCutchen.

Although, in the politics of the locker room, benching McCutchen was riskier, everyone knew he could handle it. He's a mature young man. McCutchen responded by raising his average by nearly thirty points, patrolling center field like an All-Star and maintaining a 25-30 home run pace that, if it continued, would make him an entirely different player and launch him on the road to superstardom.

As for Ronny Cedeño, he could have gone either way. In May, he went north. After batting .192 in April, Cedeño hit .286 in May and played like a winning major league shortstop. Obtaining family consensus on the Fantastic Ronny C appellation took some explanation, some persuasion and a quick trip to YouTube. It is rare that I can get an obscure 60s music reference by David. But, on May 31, when the Fantastic Ronny C finished the most encouraging month of his Pirate career by starting the come from behind rally in New York against the Mets' R.A. Dickey, a knuckleballer who had made the Bucs look silly for seven innings, we all were ready to "Bugaloo Down Broadway."

The 2011 Pittsburgh Pirates.

He can hit. He can run. He can field. He can throw. Ta-ba-ta.

Neil Walker. The Pittsburgh Kid.

Pedro.

The Legend. Garrett Freakin' Jones.

Ryan Doumit.

The Fantastic
Ronnie C.

Jeff Karstens, Charlie Morton, Paul Maholm, James McDonald and Kevin Correia. For four months, five fingers that made a fist.

Reinforcements: Alex Presley, Brad Lincoln and Derrek Lee.

Easy peasy, lemon squeezy. Joel Hanrahan and Michael McKenry.

Walk-off: Andrew McCutchen.

Adult supervision. Manager Clint Hurdle.

June:

CHAPTER ONE:

MAJOR LEAGUE

There is an old saying that when the Chicago Cubs, who have not won a World Series in over a hundred years, hand out their little pocket schedules, there is always a place at the beginning of June marked "Fold Here." On June 2, the Bucs took the kind of punch in the stomach that could make a team fold, blowing a 7-0 lead and walking in the winning run in a loss to the Mets.

Next up were the Philadelphia Phillies, Powerhouse of Pennsylvania. On the heels of the meltdown against the Mets, this was just the type of series to put the Bucs on the road to oblivion they have traveled for the past eighteen years. Plus, for the second year in a row, the Phillies brought with them nearly 20,000 fans to take over PNC Park. It was an absolutely perfect Friday night and Pirate fans came out too, including my baseball guru Jim and me along with Andee and Jim's wife, Sheryl. It was a great atmosphere for baseball, one rarely seen on a non-fireworks night in Pittsburgh, and the dueling rooting sections only added to it.

The Phillies played one of their four aces, 2008 World Series hero Cole Hamels, and he was all of that. In Hamels' eight innings, the Pirates managed only a single by Andrew

McCutchen. The Pirates countered with Jeff Karstens, the Bucs' fifth starter. Since replacing the injured Ohlendorf in the rotation, Karstens had given the Bucs a chance to win a lot of games the way a good fifth starter should, by keeping it close for five or six innings. Karstens was gritty but he was no Cole Hamels, and he was facing a full Phillies line-up, including former MVP Jimmy Rollins; All-Star second baseman Chase Utley, back from injury; the monstrous slugger Ryan Howard, who was another former MVP; and a bunch of other guys who could hit. It should have been a slaughter.

It wasn't. Karstens didn't quite match Hamels pitch for pitch but he almost matched him inning for inning. When Karstens left after seven innings the score was 1-1. To the delight of "Old John McGraw" next to me, the Bucs had manufactured the tying run without a hit—a walk to the Fantastic Ronny C, a sacrifice bunt by Karstens, a wild pitch and a sacrifice fly by Tabata. Or, as Jim put it, "get 'em on, get 'em over, get 'em in."

From there, we were on the edge of our seats. There was drama in nearly every half inning. After Overbay saved a run with a diving stop in the tenth, the Bucs almost won it in the bottom half. But Phillies third baseman Placido Polanco made a brilliant barehanded pick-up to nail Tabata by half a step as the potential winning run was crossing home plate. Four Pirate relief pitchers combined to hold the Phillies to two hits in five innings. Phillies catcher Carlos Ruiz took rookie Daniel Moskos, the player the Bucs selected fourth in the 2007 draft ahead of Matt Weiters, to the center field wall in the top of the twelfth, but Andrew McCutchen ran it down.

In the bottom of the twelfth, former Pirate reliever Danys Baez got two quick outs for the Phillies. But Xavier Paul singled to center and promptly stole second, an aggressive move since McCutchen had been gunned down in the ninth on a perfect throw by Ruiz. Then Baez went to 3-1 on Tabata. I told Jim that the Bucs were going to win on the next pitch. Jim said no way—first base was open, Tabata's run meant nothing and a rookie in his fourth game, Josh Harrison, was coming up next. Jim was right, as he always is. But the Phillies didn't figure it out either and there is something to be said for the Power of Belief. Baez gave Tabata a pitch to hit, Jose slapped it off Utley's glove into right and Xavier Paul slid home just ahead of Ruiz's tag.

It was the perfect end to a perfect night. Most of the Pirate half of the crowd stayed to stand and cheer. A few minutes later, thousands of people were streaming over the Clemente Bridge into downtown. Someday, maybe someday soon, it's going to be like that every night. When it is, they should remember this night, the night when, for the first time in a long time, the Pittsburgh Pirates were in the major leagues.

CHAPTER TWO:

PERSEVERANCE

Didn't see that one coming.

I was not alone. After taking two of three from the imposing Phillies, the Pirates squared off against another contender, the Arizona Diamondbacks. The Bucs were down 5-3 in the eighth. Kevin Correia, heroic on the road but once again struggling at home, had given up two long homers to right and Evan Meek had given up another to left. Clint Hurdle said he was close to bringing in a rookie reliever who had just arrived that afternoon. This effectively would have called it a night. Hurdle thought better of it at the last, which was a good thing.

After a lead-off double by Garrett Jones in the bottom of the eighth, Jose Tabata banged a double off the right centerfield wall to make it 5-4. Rookie infielder Josh Harrison failed twice to bunt and then laced a single up the middle and the game was tied. After the D-backs botched a bunt play and McCutchen walked, Overbay cleared the bases with another double, the third of the inning. Hanrahan then set down the shell-shocked Diamondbacks in short order and just like that the Pirates had turned their all-too-familiar three hits in the first seven innings into a sweet 8-5 win.

The late-inning reversal was another testament to perseverance for a team that has learned how to hang around in games where they are being dominated, perhaps because it happens so often. For Garrett Jones it was that and maybe a little bit more.

Garrett Jones just sort of appeared in Pittsburgh in July 2009. He already was twenty-eight years old, a career minor leaguer who had been blocked by better players in the Twins' strong minor league system. Except Garrett Jones didn't look like a career minor leaguer. He was 6-4 and nearly 250 pounds and he could run. He had a short quick left-handed stroke, the kind that looked like it could last in the majors, and, as you might expect, he could hit it far.

Three months later, Jones had hit twenty-one home runs in half a season. It appeared that the Pirates' bargain basement shopping had paid off and that they had found a real player. By the end of 2009, Jones was starting to accumulate nicknames. The Legend. GI Jones. GFJ—Garrett Freakin' Jones. In 2010, Jones hit twenty-one more homers, not at the 2009 pace but still some power on a team that had very little. More troublingly, the short quick swing was mostly gone, replaced with a longer and more looping version. At the same time, and not coincidentally, Jones started to struggle mightily with left-handed pitching.

By the beginning of 2011, Garrett Jones was a platoon player in right field. In April he was fine, with five home runs and a .265 average. Then, just as he was starting to put together a third solid season in what was becoming a career for a player who had waited so long to have one, Garrett Jones fell apart. He batted .179 in May. The month ended worse than it began and was even more painful to watch than it sounds. By early June, Jones mostly was reduced to pinch hitting. On base only a few times in June, he nevertheless already had managed to get picked off and doubled off first base in important situations. It was getting to be now or never time for Garrett Jones. Clint Hurdle made that clear—and not very delicately.

When Garrett Jones came up to pinch hit to start the Pirate eighth inning with the Bucs down 5-3, nobody expected much. They only had won a couple games all season with late rallies. But when Jones battled Diamondbacks reliever David Hernandez through eight pitches and came through with a double to right center, he gave them life. After the Pirates had rallied and the whole team was celebrating on the field, I happened to see Hurdle as he found Jones and quietly patted him on the back. Whether this was a new beginning or the last embers of a short and belated but honorable career, it was a good night for Garrett Jones and he had earned it.

CHAPTER THREE:

ADVERSITY

Oh brother.

It should have been one of the best nights of the season. After wasting another brilliant outing by Paul Maholm, six innings of one-hit pitching, giving away the lead in the eighth and falling behind in the tenth, the Bucs battled back to tie on a double by Andrew McCutchen and a single by Neil Walker. Then relief pitcher Daniel McCutchen got into and out of a huge jam in the eleventh, thanks to a slick 3-6-3 double play led by Lyle Overbay. This set the stage for a dramatic, bench-clearing, walk-off home run to lead off the bottom of the twelfth by the blazing hot Andrew McCutchen. The win brought the Bucs back to .500 at 30-30 on June 8, a plateau they had not reached this late in the season since 2005.

Early in the game, catcher Chris Snyder hit one fair down the left field line. Until Memorial Day weekend, Snyder had shared the catching with Ryan Doumit. It was unorthodox and it was expensive. It also was working. They were two thirty-year-old catchers with a lot of miles on them. The rotation was keeping them fresh. They were hitting better. Snyder always could defend and even Doumit was improved behind the plate with less wear and tear. Best of all, they were providing the stability a dramatically improved starting rotation needed.

Doumit went down at the end of May with a broken ankle. He would be gone until August. The hope was that Snyder could hold on until Doumit returned. The fear was that Snyder would wear down. A large man who had crouched for a living for a long time, Snyder had suffered from back pain all spring and had started the season on the disabled list.

This was a precarious situation and it was about to get a lot worse. As Snyder's drive caromed off the railing and bounced toward Diamondback left fielder Xavier Nady, the former Pirate whose trade to the Yankees in 2008 had yielded such a bountiful harvest, Snyder plodded on toward second. On his best day, he ran like a mule. It is unclear whether Chris Snyder got hurt because he slid so awkwardly or whether he slid so awkwardly because he already was hurt. Either way, Snyder was out by a mile and he had suffered a herniated disk. Two days later Chris Snyder had back surgery. He would be out for the season.

To make matters worse, Jason Jaramillo, the third-string catcher who had played a fair amount the past couple years, was injured too. The Pirates were down to their fourth and fifth catchers, two career minor leaguers. At best, this would add another very weak bat on a team that already had more than enough players who were not hitting.

After a superb seven shutout innings by Jeff Karstens to start the post-Snyder era, albeit a wasted one in another punchless 2-0 loss, the Pirates began a four-game series with the Mets. The opening game was the worst game the Pirates had played all season. Charlie Morton had a rough night. He also did not get any help. The Bucs were charged with two errors and they could have been charged with five. Once again, they could not score runs. It added up to an 8-1 loss.

The Pirates did not fall apart because of the fourth string catcher. Just about everyone had pitched in. There was, however, an inescapable feeling that the karma had shifted. In the context of their limited talent, the Pirates had been a very together team. They were not together on this night. It did not help that, before the game, Evan Meek, the Pirates' All-Star in 2010, once again went on the disabled list. That list now had seven important players on it. Lots of teams have injuries. Some have more. But for a team that was swimming upstream as the Pirates had been for a generation, and for once doing a good job, it didn't seem fair.

CHAPTER FOUR:
THE EDGE OF GREATNESS

I often wonder what it would have been like to have been there at the very moment when someone became truly great. The Beatles in Hamburg in 1960. F. Scott Fitzgerald when he wrote *The Great Gatsby.* Albert Einstein in 1905. Although I have never seen anything close to that magnitude, I have witnessed a few smaller and still magical emergences. I am witnessing one now.

In June of 2011 the Pirates had a player who was becoming great. For this reason, the Pirates once again did not collapse when history and circumstances suggested they would. After showing cracks in the foundation in the 8-1 pasting by the Mets, the Bucs pulled themselves together to win five of their next six games. They took two of the last three from the Mets and then went on the road to sweep the Astros in Houston. With twenty road wins already, the Bucs put the road disaster of 2010 in their rear view mirror.

Others contributed. Clint Hurdle muttered something about chicken wire and duct tape and waved away any notion of self-pity: "we're not going there." Hurdle also called this a chance for creativity by the general manager. Neal Huntington responded with a small trade for a minor league catcher to hold the fort. Fittingly, his name was Michael McKenry. He was stumpy and it didn't look like he would hit much but at least he might settle things down behind the plate.

The starting pitchers continued to excel, especially Paul Maholm and Jeff Karstens—a soft tossing lefty and an even softer tossing righty—each of whom threw seven shutout innings to account for two of those wins. Karstens was a throw-in in the Xavier Nady trade that also brought Tabata, Ohlendorf and Daniel McCutchen. For two years Karstens was an afterthought. The Pirates even released him from the forty-man roster, which made him available for any other team to sign. Now he had the fifth lowest ERA in the league and he toyed with the Astros in Houston like a young Greg Maddux.

Joel Hanrahan was anything but a soft tosser. He was blowing hitters away with ninety-nine-mile-an-hour fastballs and wicked sliders. Hanrahan was treading on hallowed ground. He drew comparisons to Rich Gossage in 1977, a season long forgotten by most but in fact the most dominant relief pitching in Pirate history, save possibly Elroy Face's unfathomable 18-1 record in 1959. And he drew them from Pirate post-game host Kent Tekulve, who was in that Pirate bullpen in 1977 and who knows something about relief pitching, having done it in the majors for more than fifteen years, including, not least, the last out against the Baltimore Orioles in the seventh game of the 1979 World Series.

The patchwork Pirates somehow found themselves at 35-33 on June 16. They even started to draw a little national press, including a long feature on the rebirth of Charlie Morton on SI.com. Morton has been terrific, even if not quite as terrific lately. But I suspect that SI.com will look back in a few years and ask how they could have been writing about Charlie Morton at the exact moment that the best Pirate player in a generation was blossoming into a superstar.

The new math websites have rated him one of the top three players in baseball. He is batting almost .500 in June. He hits home runs even though he only weighs 175 pounds. He gets his walks, too. It is hard to pitch around him. Not because there are such great hitters behind him; there aren't. Because it means that he would be running wild on the bases, where he is just starting to learn how disruptive a force he can be. He plays hard and he plays hurt. They used to say in Philadelphia that "two thirds of the earth's surface is covered by water. The rest is covered by Garry Maddox." That's the way it is in center field these days in PNC Park.

He is the kind of player who can put a team on his back. He knows how good he is and how good he is going to be. He is in the prime of youth and he carries himself like a prince.

Andrew McCutchen. Prince Andrew of Pittsburgh.

CHAPTER FIVE:
REUNION

The catching crisis continued. Chicken wire and duct tape only can take you so far. The Bucs dropped three in a row to the Indians in Cleveland and then were hammered by the Baltimore Orioles at home in the first game of a three-game series.

Actually, there was a catcher at PNC Park who was just what the Pirates needed. He hit over .300 four times for them. He was energetic and athletic and he could fill the whole stadium with his positive spirit. Unfortunately, he was sixty-seven years old.

If Manny Sanguillen's knees had paid a price for his youth, they never affected his smile. There are four monuments to the 1971 Pirates at PNC Park. Two of them are permanent, the statues of Roberto Clemente and Willie Stargell. The other two are living, Steve Blass in the broadcast booth and Manny Sanguillen on the patio behind right-center field, serving pulled pork sandwiches and signing autographed pictures at Manny's BBQ. In his way, Sangy was still helping the Bucs and they were still helping him—but he was not going to solve the great catching crisis of 2011.

He would, however, play a prominent role in the commemoration of the 1971 World Series, timed, of course, for the Orioles' visit to PNC Park. Properly done, and this one was, such events cannot simply be celebrations. They are bittersweet and they also must include the painful recognition of the passage of time. The most important people, Clemente and Stargell, were not here. Nor were Dock Ellis and Danny Murtaugh, the "Whistling Irishman," the Bucs' manager in both 1960 and 1971; and Jose Pagan, whose double drove in the thundering Stargell from first with the winning run in the seventh game, and who had passed away just a couple weeks earlier.

Clemente in particular is a distant if indelible memory. He never got old and he never will. The players who came back in 2011 did. For me, the most painful were Bruce Kison and Milt May, the heroes of the first night game in World Series history. They were boys on that 1971 team, twenty-one years old—not that much older than I was. Now they are in their sixties. There is no turning back for them, or for me.

But the haunting part is not the only part. For them, this was a chance to recall something special and a reminder that a part of it lives forever. For us, it was a chance to remember what it felt like to watch it and to be back at that point in life, a subject, you may have gathered, of considerable importance to me. There always will be a place for looking back to when people were at their best, even in the small realm of sports. It is tradition and it is part of culture.

Clint Hurdle understood this when he invited the 1971 players into the locker room before the game. We see this more in college athletics than in the sometimes jaded adult world of professional sports. For a team that is trying to learn how to compete for championships and to restore a tradition that has been lost, it was an insightful idea. There are things that only people who have done the same jobs can fully understand, like the conversation Hurdle reported during which 1971 fireballer Bob Johnson asked Joel Hanrahan about why he had thrown a 3-2 change-up the other night. If only Roberto Clemente could have sat with Andrew McCutchen and talked with him about the duties and responsibilities of greatness.

One other thing that could be said for Hurdle's idea: it worked. The Bucs snapped back from the four straight losses to take two from the Orioles, just as they had come back in the 1971 World Series. The remarkable season was holding together. They would need more than chicken wire and duct tape now, though.

The Boston Red Sox were coming to town.

CHAPTER SIX:

REVOLUTION

The best assignment I ever had in school was from Professor Robert Colodny at the University of Pittsburgh. Professor Colodny had a plate in his head from the Spanish Civil War. He was, I was once told, the last person ever brought before the House Un-American Activities Committee. Professor Colodny gave the class a list of seventeen names and asked us to write the history of twentieth century Europe. This was no small task in a time before personal computers, much less the Internet. So off to the card catalog we went and also, in my case, happily back to my old stomping grounds in the microfilm room at Carnegie Library.

As we came to learn, every one of these seventeen people had been assassinated. These murders reflected powerful forces of history, some timeless, some specific to a time of extraordinary upheaval. I do not remember all of them but every once in awhile I will hear a name and know it was from the list. Walter Rathenau. Engelbert Dollfuss. Giacomo Matteoti. Andrés Nin. Trotsky.

Recently, I read an article from *The New Republic* on another one, Rosa Luxemburg. Luxemburg was a Communist leader in Germany and elsewhere. She was first jailed and then executed in 1919 by right wing elements in post-World War I Germany, along with another member of the list, Karl Liebknecht. Wikipedia lists Luxemburg's profession as "Revolutionary" and her mother's last name, it turns out, is the same as mine.

****

Revolution was in the air as the mighty Boston Red Sox came to Pittsburgh at the end of June to take on the proletarian Pirates. The tables had turned in the more than two centuries since Lexington and Concord. The mega-market Red Sox were now the oppressors. As my sister in Boston helpfully put it as she organized a family reunion for the occasion, it was a chance to see what $300 million will buy you. This was only a small exaggeration. The Red Sox payroll was over $161 million to the Pirates $46 million. The Sox had just spent almost as much to add two superstars in the off-season, Adrian Gonzales and the presently-injured Carl Crawford, as the Pirates paid their whole team. As the Red Sox arrived in Pittsburgh, it had bought them 44-30, the second best record in baseball.

I don't love the Red Sox, but I can't hate them. My grandfather was from Boston. We have gone there since I was six years old. Memories of historic Salem and Sturbridge and the seaside

Preston Beach Motel in Swampscott, a north end town where some of our favorite cousins still live, are intertwined with the childhood thrill of watching theretofore unseen Red Sox baseball card heroes Frank Malzone and Bill Monbouquette come to life on a tiny black and white television set in 1963.

Later, from a distance, it was the Impossible Dream of 1967—the magical Triple Crown year of Carl Yastrzemski, Jim Lonborg and the young superstar in waiting, Tony Conigliaro, from near Swampscott, who would suffer a horrific beaning that summer from which he would never fully recover either in baseball or in a much-too-short life.

I was in the bleachers at Fenway on a night in 1975 when Jim Palmer mowed down Freddie Lynn and Jim Rice and the rest of them in an otherwise golden Red Sox summer, the same night I heard Jim Woods, the Possum, Bob Prince's sidekick of the 1960s, on the Red Sox post-game show, for the first time in too many years and also for the last time. Back with those same favorite cousins in 1983 to see the twilight of Yaz and then a year later with baby Lauren to introduce my grandfather's two younger brothers to the first great-grandchild of a generation.

So we had a rich and deep connection to Boston even before my sister Peggy and her family moved to Needham in

1992. My nephew and niece have lived there virtually their entire lives. I could hardly begrudge them rooting for their hometown team. They had long since earned their stripes as long-distance Pittsburgh sports fans, especially of our beloved Pitt basketball team, for whom they had traveled far and wide.

Insufferable as they recently have become, my family excepted, Red Sox fans also have paid their dues. They wandered in the wilderness without a World Championship for eighty-six years from the sell-off of Babe Ruth in 1918 until the great day arrived in 2004. They endured perhaps the most painful collapse in the history of the World Series in 1986. If the right to self-satisfaction and condescension can be honestly earned, it has been earned here.

Finally, and whatever else, the Red Sox are not the Yankees.

Nevertheless, this series would not be a love fest. In the midst of a revolutionary season, the Pirates had class warfare on their minds when the Red Sox came to town—and if they didn't, I did. The Bucs were at .500 after seventy-four games and they were only three games out of first place in the Central Division of the National League. Strange doings were afoot in Pittsburgh and, however graciously with our

Boston family in town for the occasion, we were hoping for those strange doings to continue.

****

Friday night June 24 was another milepost in the rebirth of the Pittsburgh Pirates. It was an overflow crowd, a strong and vocal majority of them Pirate fans, along with a healthy complement of New England insurgents anxious to contribute to the Pittsburgh economy. Both teams left men on the bases all night long. Paul Maholm was all over the place but once again found a way to give his team a chance to win. When Maholm departed after scuffling for five and a third, the Bucs led 2-1, to which they would add an unearned run in the bottom of the sixth.

From there, the drama was in the bullpen and it was in the seventh and eighth innings. In the seventh, rookie lefty Tony Watson pitched himself into a two-on, one-out jam. Up came Adrian Gonzales, best hitter in baseball in 2011, who had singled twice before Maholm just gave up and hit him. To a roar rarely heard in PNC Park, Watson got Gonzales to foul out to the catcher. Then Clint Hurdle brought in Daniel McCutchen, who rarely strikes out anyone, to face the ever-dangerous Kevin Youkilis, who rarely strikes out. Needless to say, Youkilis struck out and there were, as we had come to say, "three outs to Hanrahan."

Those three outs were even more stirring. With two singles and a sacrifice bunt, the Red Sox quickly had the tying runs in scoring position. They were still there with two outs when the giant slugger David Ortiz, Big Papi, relegated to pinch hitting by the absence of the designated hitter, strode to the plate against Jose Veras. To that point, it had rained four times, each of them a pleasant early summer mist. Rain number five was the real thing and it turned this climactic at-bat into a scene from a B-grade sports movie. By the time the torrent slowed down there were two strikes on the mighty Ortiz. Papi battled bravely to foul off pitch after pitch and keep more than 39,000 fans on the edge of their seats, from which they exploded when Ortiz finally grounded sharply to the Fantastic Ronny C to end the threat.

Even with the top of the order, there would be no such drama in the ninth. It was Hammer Time. After three quick and painless outs, the last of which was against Gonzales, Joel Hanrahan had converted his twenty-first consecutive save opportunity. The Pittsburgh Pirates at 38-37 once again had fought back to a winning record. They had done this without hitting a home run in the past seven games. They had done this by playing a cleaner and more focused game than the Boston Red Sox.

****

It was a sweet night with just a bit of sadness. Although the larger family reunion would be Sunday, this would be the last game for a while, maybe a long while, with just Rachel and me. Rachel was moving away, to College Station, Texas of all places. Rachel was leaving for a great opportunity and with a great guy, to whom Rachel would become engaged the following winter.

I struggled with the move at first. Rachel has been in Pittsburgh. Even though she has been on her own, she has been such a daily part of our lives. I would miss everything—her smile, her laughter, her wit, her encyclopedic knowledge and total recall of a vast array of subjects, her artist's perspective and her unique ability, since she was a small child, to see the most interesting things that everyone else misses. I would miss Mark, too, especially his economist's insights on the business of sports, a topic of interest to me and any baseball fan in Pittsburgh, and on the games, too.

Rachel moving 1500 miles away was going to be hard. But I came around, and not just because I had to. When all was said and done, Rachel believes this is the right move and I believe in Rachel. She is a constant source of joy and an even deeper source of pride.

With each child there are special things. Rachel and I share a love for the silliest lines from a wide array of movies. I told Rachel that stumpy Pirate catcher Michael McKenry reminded me of Eddie, the truant school age caddie in *The Greatest Game Ever Played*, a film starring Shia LeBeouf about Francis Ouimet's shocking win as an amateur in the U.S. Open of 1913. Rachel has no interest in golf and if she had ever seen this movie, I was not aware of it. I just knew, though, when Rachel laughed at the sight of little Michael McKenry ambling toward the mound, that the next words out of her mouth would be the classic line from that movie. It was the greatest of a series of cornball lines delivered by little Eddie as he calms the brave Ouimet, just as Michael McKenry would be out all night to calm down the Pirate pitchers who towered over him.

"Easy peasy, lemon squeezy."

Just like the Bucs over the Red Sox. It is always that way with Rachel. I will miss her terribly and when I think of her, I will smile.

****

It was a good weekend for the revolution. The Pirates split the next two with the Red Sox to take the series, winning a 6-4 home run derby on Saturday night during which I learned that my Boston nephew Dan in fact was all Pirates and his sister Julie was at least ambivalent. The game featured a three-run bomb by the long-dormant Lyle Overbay and a solo shot by Garrett Jones that trumped three Red Sox homers, all with the bases empty. Overbay hit his homer off forty-four-year-old Red Sox knuckleballer Tim Wakefield. As a twenty-five-year-old converted infielder who had learned how to throw a knuckleball, Wakefield almost had pitched the Bucs to the World Series in 1992. Nineteen years later, except for a guy who pitched two innings, he was the last player in baseball who had ever played on a winning team for the Pittsburgh Pirates.

****

Sunday afternoon was the reunion. With Andee's brilliant planning and precise execution, we were able to get four grandparents ages seventy-eight through ninety-three in and out of a record crowd of 39,511 at PNC Park in only eight and a half hours. Had the Pirates been as efficient, they might have swept the mighty Red Sox. However, as my dad pointed out, more than once, you can't win making four errors.

Especially after Jose Tabata went down like he was shot after beating out a bunt to lead off the first, making three of eight starters on the disabled list. We did get to see David Ortiz hit one four miles out of PNC Park but just foul, as well as an odd little brush back war between teams that play each other three games every few years. It was a long day and a frustrating 4-2 loss but it also featured our entire family, all three generations, and guest appearances by a few cousins. Lauren and Nick even came in from Chicago. Who knows how many more days like this we all will have together. Thanks to my sister we had this one.

CHAPTER SEVEN:

MIDSEASON REPORT

By the end of June, after taking two of three against Joey Bats and the Blue Jays in Toronto, the Pirates had clinched a winning record at midseason. The Bucs were two games out of first place in the National League Central. Tempting as it is to conclude the midseason report with these two stunning facts, this remarkable season deserves more than that. Here goes:

The Manager

We have to start with this. Managers aren't supposed to matter this much in baseball. But does anyone think the Pirates would be winning if they hadn't changed managers?

The HBO series, *Band of Brothers*, tracks Easy Company as it paratroops into Normandy and fights its way through France and Belgium and into Germany to save the world. The most compelling parts of a very powerful series are the interviews with the actual soldiers whose heroics are portrayed by young actors. The leader of the Band of Brothers was Major Richard Winters. At the end of an early episode, Major Winters, then in his eighties, and who has since passed away, appeared briefly on screen. He was very quiet and plain spoken. A friend who also saw it had the same reaction I did.

Some people just have "it."

This is only baseball. But Clint Hurdle has it. Especially for this team.

The All-Stars

On the field, it starts with two players who are All-Stars, whether or not they are selected. Andrew McCutchen is, simply, one of the best and most complete players in baseball. You only start eight players. It is a very good thing when one of them is great.

It also is a very good thing to have a closer. In the first half of 2011, with no warning, Joel Hanrahan has been the best closer in baseball, which is a huge credit to General Manager Neal Huntington. Acquired in a seemingly minor trade in late 2009, Hanrahan has developed into a dominant force. So much of the psychology of the Pirates in 2011 has been to try to get a lead, any lead, and get the game to Joel Hanrahan. When they do that, they don't lose. The other team knows it too.

The Starting Pitching

No big names. No ace. Just five fingers that make a fist. Every one of them—Correia, Maholm, Karstens, Morton and McDonald—gives them a chance to win almost every time out. Except McDonald, who has only been good, each has had a stretch when he has been great. It is hard to single out one but if I had to it would be Jeff Karstens. Karstens has the weakest stuff, in the traditional sense. The traditional sense is mistaken. It does not consider artistry.

Except for Correia, all of them were on a staff that was an absolute disaster in 2010. Actually, they were a disaster for most of 2010. The 2010 season was so far gone that few noted that they started to get better late in the year when Ray Searage was named the pitching coach. Searage was retained to little note for 2011. Everyone knows it now. His staff has pitched a lot of innings, too many for the younger ones. It will take all of Ray Searage's skill, and maybe some reinforcements, to hold it together.

The Near Stars

Before the season, it was the four—McCutchen, Alvarez, Walker and Tabata. McCutchen has taken a big step forward. Alvarez has taken a huge step back, hitting miserably and then missing two months with a pulled muscle. He seems like a good kid and a smart kid. Whether he figures anything out this summer will go a long way to decide whether this has been fun or if it can be a season people will talk about for a long time.

In the middle are Neil Walker and Jose Tabata. They are not McCutchen, and their batting averages are well down from last year, but they are helping this team win. They play hard. Tabata gets on base and Walker drives in runs. They are strong in the field; Walker is far better at second base than most experts had expected, even if the new-world stats don't agree. There is delicacy here too. They need to find a way to get Walker some rest and to keep Tabata on the field.

The Middle Relief

For a guy who has taken a lot of criticism, some of it justified, Neal Huntington has shown a pretty consistent ability to take a bunch of no-names and scrap heap guys and make a bullpen. And then start over and do it again the next year. This year it has been Jose Veras, Chris Resop, Daniel McCutchen, Tony Watson, Danny Moskos and some others in and out. The only one anybody really heard of before the season was Moskos, and that was only because a lot of people wanted to execute David Littlefield for drafting him over

Matt Weiters. They have done it without last year's All-Star eighth inning man, Evan Meek. It helps that all they need to do is get to Hanrahan. It helps that the starters usually get through the sixth or seventh. However they are doing it, it is working and it has worked most of the time for half a season.

The Fantastic Ronny C

Since the moment Ronny Cedeño got here, there has been a loud and persistent chorus of Pirate fans demanding a trade for a shortstop. For two years, with good reason. Even now, Ronny Cedeño continues to do things, like not running out a hit or bunting with the bases loaded, which bring down the long arm of the law and get him benched for a game or two. In between, though, the Fantastic Ronny C is doing it. Almost all the time on defense where, in his own Ronny Cedeño way, he has stabilized the infield like a good shortstop should. Not too bad on offense either, as shortstops go. There are positions where the Pirates have been winning and others, most notably first base and third base, where they have been losing. For the past two months, unbeknownst to most of their fans, the Pirates have been winning at shortstop.

The Catchers

There certainly have been enough of them, seven so far. The main tandem, Chris Snyder and Ryan Doumit, was a productive team, on offense and defense. Then, in a disastrous fortnight, they were both gone. It took some rooting around but they came up with Michael McKenry. McKenry is hitting all of a buck ninety-five. It doesn't matter. He can play catcher and, for a team built on pitching, he is what they need.

The Calvary

With all of the injuries, almost half the roster is different than it was when the season began. Players just seem to come and go. But just about all of them, the infielders—Steve Pearce, Brandon Wood, Josh Harrison, Chase D'Arnaud—and the outfielders—Xavier Paul and Alex Presley—have helped them win games. One of them, and my money is on Presley, is going to need to end up being a very key player on this team.

The Third Way

There are a few ways to keep this going or even to kick it into a higher gear. One way is to get some guys back healthy and producing, especially Alvarez, Tabata, Doumit and Meek. Another way would be to spin a big trade, which is easier said than done. There is a third way. It is for three guys who can do more to step up. Garrett Jones, Lyle Overbay and Matt Diaz. They are veterans. As they head into the dog days and, heaven forbid, some meaningful late-season games, they need to play like veterans.

It is the end of June. Pigs are flying. The team that was 57-105 in 2010 is 41-39.

CHAPTER EIGHT:

FRACTURED

June 1971 also ended well for the Pirates. By midseason, the 1971 Pirates had pulled out to a 49-29 record and a two-game lead over the New York Mets in the National League East. Willie Stargell hit eleven more home runs and Dock Ellis won six more games. The Bucs had five regulars —Clemente, Stargell, Sanguillen, Hebner and Cash—hitting over .300 at the end of June.

June 1971 did not end well for me. I do not have a particularly high pain threshold or any other form of physical courage. But there have been only two events in my life where I can close my eyes and remember pain that still takes my breath away. When I was five years old I climbed up the high diving board at Parkway Cabana Club and fell back on my head on the concrete. Although, as you might imagine, this caused quite a stir from the snack bar all the way to the tetherball court, not to mention unhinging my parents, I was remarkably unharmed. I was taken for x-rays of my brain, where, as the old saying goes, they found nothing. Still, if there is anything here you think is a little bit off…

The other was the night in late June 1971 when I broke my arm punching that kid on a bicycle. My arm was just kind of hanging there and it felt like it was frozen. That hurt more than enough but that is not the pain I remember. At the hospital, the nurse who took me in to have my arm set rammed my elbow against the door and I almost passed out. Then the doctor snapped the bones into place, set my arm in a cast to my shoulder and sent me on my way for the next eight weeks.

I would not be going to summer camp. This was not the worst thing that ever happened to anyone, but it was a crushing blow to me. I had gone to this camp, outside Scranton, for two months every summer since 1966. It was a huge part of my life and, almost forty years after it closed in 1973, it still is.

I see it in my own children. There are times when only mom will do. My mom was very helpful that night. We talked about things I could do to get through the summer. We made a plan to go see Vida Blue in Cleveland. Vida Blue was a thunderbolt in the spring of 1971. He was twenty-one years old and at the end of June it looked like he would win thirty games. He didn't and we never made that trip. I don't know if my mom ever intended to go. I have never asked. It was enough that she said she would go on a night I needed to hear that. When you are fourteen years old and you want to be on your own, as much as you don't want to admit it, there are times when you need your parents. For me, this was one of those times. I didn't always count on them for the little things, but I knew that I could count on them for the big things.

Instead, it was very quickly the Pirates. I started to go to games by myself. The Pirates were hot and they were starting to pull away. On Friday night, July 9, I took my parents to see the Pirates play the Atlanta Braves.

One of the players we saw that night was Henry Aaron. I have a higher regard for Barry Bonds than most people have, including just about anyone in Pittsburgh. There was a time when I would hope that Barry Bonds could reach 500 home runs and get his due, in the historical sense, for the great player that he was. Then absurd things started to happen. Whether it was a juiced ball, juiced players or whatever, I will leave to the conscience of Barry Bonds and of baseball. I only know that the true home run king is Henry Aaron.

I saw Hank Aaron play many times. I brought a movie camera to Forbes Field one day in April 1970. I only shot about three minutes worth and the camera jumps all over the place, but I did get footage of both Aaron and Clemente. If I had kept the camera rolling, I would have a personal film record of Willie Stargell hitting one over the right field roof at Forbes Field.

I never saw any of Hank Aaron's 755 home runs in person although, oddly, I did see one by his little brother Tommy, who hit all of fourteen. It was the day after I shot my little movie, and, as the friend I went with quickly reminded me when I saw him recently for the first time in nearly forty years, the day we almost were kicked out of the tiny third deck at Forbes Field for shooting peanut shells down on the unsuspecting people below.

My behavior had improved by 1971. I wanted to show my parents the special team I had been watching. The Pirates did not disappoint. The middle of the line-up went like this: Clemente, 2 for 4. Stargell, 3 for 4 with his twenty-ninth homer and four RBIs. Hebner, 3 for 5 with a homer. Robertson, 2 for 4. Sanguillen, 3 for 5 and four RBIs. What we would not do for even one of these hitters now.

For all the offense, the thing I remember most was on defense. We sat on the third base side and it happened right in front of us. In the seventh inning, with runners on first and second, one of the Braves hit a sharp grounder to third. Richie Hebner tagged third, fired to Dave Cash at second who then threw on to Robertson at first. Tic-tac-toe, a triple play, the only one I have ever seen in person.

When it was all done it was 11-2 and the Pirates led the National League East by eight games. Clearly, if I was going to spend a summer at Three Rivers Stadium, I had picked the right summer to do it.

1971 PITTSBURGH PIRATES 1971

FRONT ROW, seated, left to right: Vic Davalillo, Jose Pagan, Coach Bill Virdon, Coach Don Leppert, Coach Frank Oceak, Manager Danny Murtaugh, Coach Don Osborn, Coach Dave Ricketts, Steve Blass and Manny Sanguillen.

MIDDLE ROW, standing, left to right: Team Physician Dr. Joseph Finegold, Trainer Tony Bartirome, Bill Mazeroski, Jackie Hernandez, Dave Cash, Gene Alley, Gene Clines, Willie Stargell, Dave Giusti, Al Oliver, Luke Walker, Charlie Sands, Traveling Secretary John Fitzpatrick and Equipment Manager John Hallahan.

TOP ROW, standing, left to right: Jim Nelson, Milt May, Bob Moose, Nelson Briles, Jim "Mudcat" Grant, Bob Veale, Bob Johnson, Dock Ellis, Bob Robertson, Rich Hebner, and Roberto Clemente.

Champions.

The Great Roberto Clemente.

Willie the Starge.

Al Oliver, the underappreciated star, hit over .300 eleven times and made seven All-Star teams.

The Gravedigger, Richie Hebner.

Bob Robertson,
The Mt. Savage
Strongboy.

Sangy.

Strength up the middle: Dave Cash, Rennie Stennett and Jackie Hernandez.

The Gunner: Bob Prince.

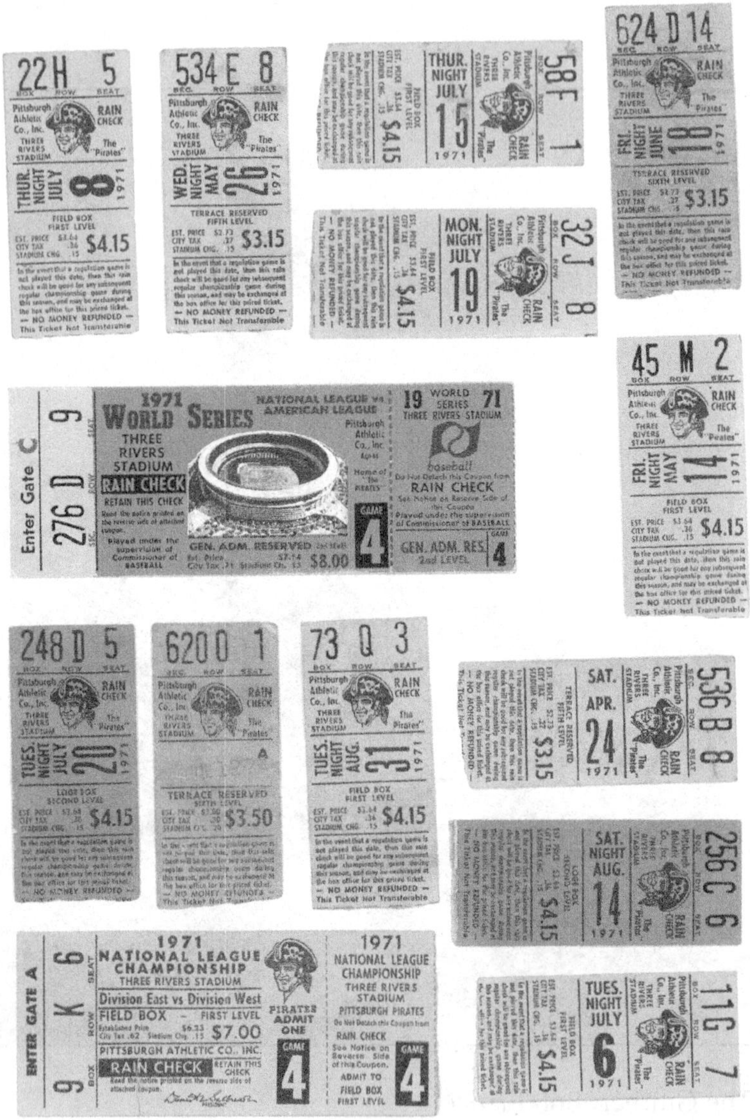
22H 5
RAIN CHECK
THUR. NIGHT JULY 8 1971
FIELD BOX FIRST LEVEL
$4.15
534 E 8
RAIN CHECK
WED. NIGHT MAY 26 1971
TERRACE RESERVED FIFTH LEVEL
$3.15
THUR. NIGHT JULY 15 1971
58 F 1
$4.15
624 D 14
RAIN CHECK
FRI. NIGHT JUNE 18 1971
TERRACE RESERVED SIXTH LEVEL
$3.15
MON. NIGHT JULY 19 1971
32 J 8
$4.15
1971 WORLD SERIES
THREE RIVERS STADIUM
NATIONAL LEAGUE vs AMERICAN LEAGUE
RAIN CHECK
Enter Gate C
276 D 9
GEN. ADM. RESERVED
$8.00
GAME 4
19 WORLD SERIES 71
GEN. ADM. RES. 2nd LEVEL
45 M 2
RAIN CHECK
FRI. NIGHT MAY 14 1971
FIELD BOX FIRST LEVEL
$4.15
248 D 5
TUES. NIGHT JULY 20 1971
LOGE BOX SECOND LEVEL
$4.15
620 O 1
TERRACE RESERVED
$3.50
73 Q 3
TUES. NIGHT AUG. 31 1971
FIELD BOX FIRST LEVEL
$4.15
SAT. APR. 24 1971
536 B 8
TERRACE RESERVED FIFTH LEVEL
$3.15
SAT. NIGHT AUG. 14 1971
256 C 6
$4.15
1971 NATIONAL LEAGUE CHAMPIONSHIP
THREE RIVERS STADIUM
Division East vs Division West
FIELD BOX - FIRST LEVEL
$7.00
PITTSBURGH ATHLETIC CO., INC.
RAIN CHECK
ENTER GATE A
9 K 6
PIRATES ADMIT ONE
GAME 4
TUES. NIGHT JULY 6 1971
11 G 7
$4.15

225 N 6
SUN. JULY 18 1971
RAIN CHECK
$4.15
PITTSBURGH ATHLETIC CO., Inc.
THREE RIVERS STADIUM
FIELD BOX — 1st LEVEL
$3.6825
25 P 8
SEPT. 4 1971
Plan "C"
NO MONEY REFUNDED
13A 4
Pittsburgh Athletic Co., Inc.
RAIN CHECK
THREE RIVERS STADIUM
The "Pirates"
TUES. NIGHT AUG. 17 1971
FIELD BOX FIRST LEVEL
$4.15
— NO MONEY REFUNDED —
This Ticket Not Transferable
1 H 6
WED. NIGHT AUG. 11 1971
$4.15
42 B 15
SUN. MAY 16 1971
$4.15
638 K 3
SUN. MAY 2 1971
TERRACE RESERVED SIXTH LEVEL
$3.15
69 N 5
WED. NIGHT JULY 7 1971
$4.15
636 C 17
SAT. NIGHT MAY 15 1971
$3.15
256 C 5
SAT. NIGHT AUG. 14 1971
LOGE BOX SECOND LEVEL
$4.15
64 A 6
MON. MAY 31 1971
$4.15
ENTER GATE A
9 L 6
1971 NATIONAL LEAGUE CHAMPIONSHIP
THREE RIVERS STADIUM
FIELD BOX — FIRST LEVEL
Division East vs Division West
$7.00
RAIN CHECK
PITTSBURGH ATHLETIC CO. INC.
PIRATES ADMIT ONE
3
634 N 8
WED. NIGHT JUNE 23 1971
$3.15
MON. AUG. 30 1971
RAIN CHECK
001414
Enter Gate 642 N 18
1971 WORLD SERIES
NATIONAL LEAGUE vs AMERICAN LEAGUE
THREE RIVERS STADIUM
RAIN CHECK
RETAIN THIS CHECK
TERRACE RESERVED
$10.00
GAME 5
19 WORLD SERIES 71
THREE RIVERS STADIUM
baseball
RAIN CHECK
TERRACE RES. 6th LEVEL
5

The Doctor. Dock Ellis did not waste his talent in 1971.

Bob Veale. Radio ball.

A tough mind-set
and a palm ball.
Dave Guisti,
the closer.

Bruce Kison and Nellie Briles and the things you can never take away: Wins over the Orioles in the 1971 World Series.

The left side of a World Championship infield: Don Hoak, The Tiger, and MVP Dick Groat.

The Cobra:
Dave Parker.

The young
Barry Bonds.

3:36 PM, October 13, 1960.

Honus Wagner.

The celebrations of the 1971 and 1979 World Championships.

The Great One. Roberto Clemente's 3,000th hit.

July:

CHAPTER ONE:

ROAD TRIP

Fourth of July weekend began, appropriately, with a trip to our nation's capital, to visit with Nick's family and watch the Bucs play the Washington Nationals. Like me, Lauren has been very fortunate in her choice of in-laws. This is not surprising since, also like me, she has been very fortunate in her choice of spouses. As has Nick, I might add.

The game was played at the Nationals' new stadium. I love going to different stadiums. Perhaps I should be embarrassed to say that I feel about them as others do when they visit churches and museums, but I'm not.

It was a breezy summer night, a perfect night for baseball. There was only one problem. All of the games we have watched with Nick's family have been the same—very close, very exciting and, at the very end the Pittsburgh team loses in the most painful way. This one was not as bad as the last, just a few months earlier and a few blocks away at the Verizon Center, a devastating loss in the NCAA basketball tournament by our Pitt Panthers to Butler on a foul committed 90 feet from the basket with less than a second to play.

This time it was just one baseball game in July, a 2-1 loss in the bottom of the ninth after forty-three-year-old former Pirate Matt Stairs hit a pinch-hit single off the right field wall. There also was a feeling of inevitability, even after an inspiring performance by Chris Resop, who came into a tie game with two on and nobody out in the eighth and struck out the side.

The Pirates were undermanned. Four of the eight position players and three of the five relief pitchers had just come up from the minors. It also turned out that the Fantastic Ronny C played the last five innings with a concussion that would put him on the disabled list for most of July. With as little as they were getting from the veterans at first base and right field, the Pirate offense truly was becoming, as one blogger aptly summarized, "Andrew McCutchen vs. the World."

All teams have injuries, but not like this. After all of the bungling, for so many years, it would be sad and ironic if the one Pirate season in this century that was worth watching was derailed by something totally beyond their control.

CHAPTER TWO:
STUMPY

There are wins and there are wins.

The Pirates did not crumble without the Fantastic Ronny C. Instead, they plugged in yet another recent minor league call-up at shortstop, Chase d'Arnaud, and took two of the last three from the Nats in D.C. Then the Bucs came home and took two out of three from the Astros. On the Fourth of July, at Andee's startling request, we bought standing-room-only tickets and stood under the scoreboard in center field at PNC Park for three hours as Paul Maholm overcame some shoddy fielding to win 5-3. The next night, my dad and I were treated to another pitching gem by the increasingly marvelous Jeff Karstens who, along with Lyle Overbay, also executed a perfect suicide squeeze.

Many experts questioned whether the Pirates could keep this up. I knew what they meant. Every time the Bucs lost a game I thought they were going to lose ten. When you are winning more on attitude and karma than talent and execution, you never know when the clock might strike midnight.

It would not be on July 8.

The Cubs came to PNC Park to start the last series before the All-Star break. There was a sellout crowd, which, sadly, did not include us, and an electric atmosphere. Watching at home, most of the night was an exercise in frustration. Aramis Ramirez, still a very sore subject for Pirate fans many years after the Bucs dumped him for a bag of balls, homered for the Cubs in the first. The Bucs battled back to lead 2-1 on a two-run infield single by Neil Walker. The Bucs blew that lead and, after Andrew McCutchen bailed them out with a homer that tied the game in the sixth, they fell behind again in the eighth. The Pirates missed chance after chance. They hit into three double plays. The karma was starting to slip away.

Every once in a while an inning warrants play-by-play to make sure all the heroes get their due. Here goes:

The bottom of the eighth, the Bucs are down 4-3 and big lefty Sean Marshall is in for the Cubs. Matt Diaz, improved of late, works a lead-off walk. Pedro Ciriaco pinch runs, which turns out to be crucial. McCutchen flies out and Walker hits a double play ball that should have ended the inning. But Ciriaco, who can run with anyone, even McCutchen, flies into second, breaks up the double play and keeps it alive. Lyle Overbay, also showing a pulse in recent days, gets his second hit to move Walker to second with the tying run.

Cubs manager Mike Quade has seen enough. He knows this is the ballgame. He calls for his closer, Carlos Marmol, even though it is only the eighth.

Marmol has not been scored upon in thirteen appearances. But on Marmol's very first pitch, Josh Harrison, acquired from the Cubs and recently brought up from the minors, repays his former team with a single to right center, his third hit of the night, on his twenty-fourth birthday, to score Walker and tie the game. This brings a big smile to Harrison's face and brings up Michael McKenry, another recent minor league call-up. McKenry is almost as wide as he is tall. I call him Stumpy except when my wife makes me call him Michael. Marmol gets ahead 0-2 and for some reason insists on continuing to throw fastballs down the middle. McKenry fouls off five in a row. It appears unthinkable to Marmol that Stumpy is capable of hitting his first major league home run off anything he can throw, even a hanging slider.

Marmol is wrong.

The TV announcers say it is the loudest they have ever heard it at PNC Park. In the left field stands there is a group of teenagers. They are holding up two signs. The first one says, "We have been waiting our whole lives for this." The second one says, "Literally, our whole lives."

CHAPTER THREE:

ALL-STAR BREAK

National League Central				
Team	**W**	**L**	**Pct.**	**GB**
Milwaukee	49	43	.533	-
St. Louis	49	43	.533	-
Pittsburgh	47	43	.522	1
Cincinnati	45	47	.489	4
Chi. Cubs	37	55	.402	12
Houston	30	62	.326	19

There is nothing like a pennant race. Nothing.

CHAPTER FOUR:

HEROES

I watched the end of this year's All-Star game with an old summer camp friend with whom I recently had reconnected. I had not seen him since 1972, the year he came to watch the Pirates play the Big Red Machine in the National League playoffs. We have much in common and we picked up like it was yesterday.

We agreed that the All-Star game was not what it used to be. Having grown up in Philadelphia, he recalled the dramatic three-run homer by the Phillies' Johnny Callison that won the All-Star game for the National League in 1964, shortly after Jim Bunning's perfect game on Father's Day. It was before the epic collapse of the 1964 Phillies who, after a dream season not unlike the one I am watching now, blew a six and a half game lead with twelve games to play when Gene Mauch panicked and started pitching Bunning and Chris Short on two days rest.

I remember Johnny Callison's home run very well. It was off Dick "The Monster" Radatz of the Red Sox. I was on my next-door neighbor's patio. It was, I am certain, one of the last All-Star games played in the afternoon. I was seven years old.

****

When you are seven years old, everyone on your team is a hero. Some may be greater heroes than others but they all are heroes. Not just the players, but anyone associated with the team.

I do not know if the Pirates have a traveling secretary today. If they do, I do not know who it is. I do not know what a traveling secretary does. But I do know that in the 1960s the traveling secretary of the Pittsburgh Pirates was Bob Rice and, as far as I was concerned, that made him a great man. I also know that there was a woman named Sally O'Leary who worked for the Pirates in the 1960s and who, I understand, still works for the Pirates. I know that she had something to do with those little bats they sold and with Prize Day and that made her a great woman, which she undoubtedly is.

The Pirates team physician was Dr. Joseph Feingold. This important fact was specified on virtually every Pirate broadcast of the 1960s. Dr. Feingold, too, was a great man. Not just because he was the Pirates' team physician, although that would have been reason enough. Because he was, as I recall it, the man who arranged the Rodef Shalom Congregation Father, Son and Daughter event after Sunday School one morning forty-six years ago. It was not an elaborate affair. Just a young man sitting in a chair in the middle of a reception hall and a long line of girls and boys politely waiting to meet him. I don't even think that there were any refreshments.

****

There are only a few things that transport you instantly back in time. This is one of them. It is not an ancient Olduvai handaxe or a Clovis spear point or any other of the hundred objects from which the BBC has told the history of the world, as Rachel recently has alerted me. Instead, it is an historical artifact of more recent vintage. It is an envelope from the Rodef Shalom Congregation Father, Son and Daughter event in 1965. On the front there is a request to donate to NEED, the Negro Emergency Education Drive, which, I have learned, has provided nearly $20 million in grant allocations to worthy African-American students in Pittsburgh since its inception in 1963. On the back there is this:

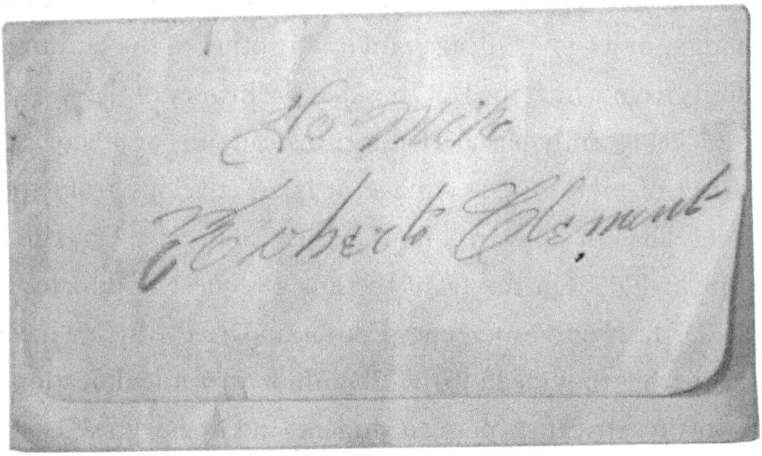
Robert Clement

CHAPTER FIVE:
PRIDE

If it had not happened earlier it surely would have happened on January 1, 1973, the morning I grabbed the *Pittsburgh Post-Gazette*, took it up to my bedroom and, like every person in Pittsburgh and every baseball fan in the world, read in stunned disbelief that Roberto Clemente was missing in a plane crash on a humanitarian mission and believed to be dead. Had there been any question that it would be the Clemente Bridge, that the right field wall in PNC Park would be the Clemente Wall and that it would be 21 feet high, that for the Pittsburgh Pirates there would be Roberto Clemente and there would be everyone else, those questions went away on January 1, 1973.

But it happened earlier.

Roberto Clemente turned thirty-seven years old in 1971. He had been a transcendent player for a long time. He had gradually and in some quarters grudgingly become a hero and perhaps even a legend. In 1971, he became a god.

It had been a long hard road. The first great Latin American player and everything that came with it. The language barrier that never went away. The claim that he was a malingerer.

The pride. Roberto Clemente was not without his imperfections. It would never be easy with him. I remember all of it, but from a child's perspective. Others have researched and written it better than I could.

In the summer of 1971 Pittsburgh opened its heart to Roberto Clemente. For the country, it may not have been until the World Series that fall. For Pittsburgh, it was earlier. I do not need to research this. I was there, and I was old enough to know.

Roberto Clemente had been beloved by many people in Pittsburgh for a long time, especially by children. But a number of things came together in 1971 that took the way Pittsburgh felt about Roberto Clemente to a higher and more lasting place. Some involved him only indirectly. There was a new stadium with, however briefly, an exciting new feel to it, just as the Pirates, with their fancy new double knit uniforms, were putting together their best team in a long time—and maybe their best team ever.

When Pittsburgh took another look at Roberto Clemente in 1971, it began to have a feeling that doesn't happen much anymore, especially in places like Pittsburgh. The feeling a city develops for the baseball player who stays for his whole career. Ted Williams in Boston. Ernie Banks in Chicago.

When it begins to realize that it better appreciate him now because it will not have him forever.

For me, the defining memory of how Pittsburgh felt about Roberto Clemente was in what ended up as an 8-7 ten-inning loss to the San Francisco Giants at Three Rivers Stadium on July 22, 1971. It was a sunny Thursday afternoon. We were sitting on first base, behind the Pirate dugout. My friend at the Webster Hall Hotel had done me well that day. Clemente was getting a day off. The Bucs went into the ninth inning down 7-3 to Juan Marichal, which was not a good place to be. But after three singles and a walk it was 7-5. The Giants brought in Steve Hamilton to pitch.

To the sounds of "Jesus Christ Superstar," which is what they played when he came to bat in 1971, and which itself tells you all you need to know, Roberto Clemente came up to pinch hit. He was greeted with a thunderous standing ovation from the crowd of 33,000. A moment later, when Clemente bounced a double over third to tie the game, there was another thunderous standing ovation. Jackie Hernandez came in to run for Clemente. As he came off the field, there was a yet another thunderous standing ovation.

It took far too long for some, but the people of Pittsburgh knew what they had in Roberto Clemente and they knew it before his plane went down and he was gone.

****

When Roberto Clemente came to the plate, he would twirl his neck in exaggerated circles to loosen up an old and severe injury. After he was settled in, which took a while, and found a pitch he liked, Clemente would uncoil and dive across the plate to drive the ball into right field. He was the complete player and the complete player would use the whole field. Nobody ever did this more explosively, more fearlessly or with more passion. Although he sometimes rocked back and wound up on an inside pitch to drive it to left, Clemente's opposite field approach to hitting meant that he would not hit as many home runs. This is the one thing that the few holdouts cite to deny Roberto Clemente his place among the greatest of the great.

The way Roberto Clemente attacked the strike zone also led, not infrequently, to one of the dramatic moments in baseball: Roberto Clemente escaping a brush back pitch. The batting helmet would come off, dirt would fly everywhere and, it seemed, Clemente would move in three directions at once. Then he would slowly pick himself up, dust himself off, adjust his batting helmet and give the pitcher the most serious and ominous look. I'm sure that Roberto Clemente did not lace one up the middle past the pitcher's ear every single time this happened. I just remember it that way.

On the bases, Clemente ran with a wild galloping style. When he arrived to beat a throw as he so often did it was to a tremendous commotion. That style masked the fact that Clemente was a consummately intelligent base runner. The single into a double. The double into a triple, eighty-five of them after the age of thirty.

Roberto Clemente also was the greatest defensive right fielder who ever played baseball, about which there is no serious debate. If it was easy, it was the basket catch, same as the greatest centerfielder, Willie Mays, but with, if you are allowed to say this, a little extra Latin flair and a looping underhanded toss back to the infield. If it was hard, it was like watching a bird in flight. Everyone has a favorite Clemente catch. There was one in Houston that is mythological. For me, when I close my eyes, I see myself in the right field seats at Three Rivers Stadium with my father on July 18, 1971, looking down on Roberto Clemente as he flew into right center to make a diving backhanded grab to save the first game of a double-header sweep over the Dodgers, before Luke Walker took a no-hitter into the ninth in the second game.

And then there was The Arm.

Words can only take this so far. Do yourself a favor. Get a hold of some old tapes or online videos. Rockets to third base coming out of nowhere from the right field bullpen at Forbes Field. Behind the runner who took a wide turn at first. Or just to throw someone out at first on a sharp hit. In fifty years of watching baseball I have seen one throw by anybody else that I would call a Roberto Clemente throw, by Jose Guillen from the right field wall to third base one night in Colorado.

There are countless candidates, but, for me, there is one Clemente throw that stands above all others. It is odd that this throw is not better known because it prevented the winning run from scoring in the bottom of the ninth inning of one of the truly great World Series games, the sixth game of the 1971 World Series, won 3-2 by the Orioles in the tenth by Frank Robinson's daring slide under the leaping Manny Sanguillen. Somehow this throw did not make the Clemente highlight reel so frequently shown from that World Series, perhaps because there is so much from which to choose. For me, this would have been the first shot, a jolt to sit up straight and pay attention because something special is coming, like the first thundering drum beat in "Like a Rolling Stone."

With the score tied at two, and Mark Belanger on first, Don Buford hits one down the right field line to the wall. There are two outs and Belanger is running; Buford's hit surely will win the game. Clemente sails over to the deepest corner, plays the carom perfectly in an unfamiliar stadium, grabs the ball, wheels and fires from the right field wall, 300 feet away. An instant later, it takes a short hop and hits Manny Sanguillen's catcher's mitt at home plate. Sangy does not move a muscle. Neither does Belanger at third. They showed this throw on the World Series highlight film at our camp the next summer. The Pittsburgh and Baltimore kids knew it was coming. Everyone else just gasped. I know that this is the greatest throw Roberto Clemente ever made because it is the greatest throw that anyone ever made.

Roberto Clemente also hit a home run and a triple in that sixth game. The next day he hit another home run, 400 feet to dead center, to break a scoreless tie in the taut and excruciating 2-1 seventh game win. It was his twelfth hit in a World Series in which he batted .414 and hit in every game, and in which he played right field and ran the bases in a way that the people who saw it will never forget, the way people in Pittsburgh had seen it for seventeen years and I had seen it all that summer. Afterward, interviewed for television in the locker room, he put aside the praise that was being heaped upon him to thank his mother and father in Spanish. Roberto Clemente was an artist and the 1971 World Series was his masterpiece.

Life works in strange ways. I wasn't even supposed to be there. It was only because I did a stupid kid thing and broke my arm. Forty years later, it is one of the treasures of my life. In the summer of 1971, at the exact moment of his apotheosis, I watched the great Roberto Clemente play baseball.

CHAPTER SIX:

RELEVANCE

Just as the baseball world rediscovered Roberto Clemente in 1971, so too would it rediscover the Pittsburgh Pirates in July 2011.

The All-Star break is a traditional point for taking stock. When the national media took their first serious look at the 2011 Pirates, the consensus was that it was a heartwarming but unsustainable story. As one of the national writers put it, give or take, the Pirates were headed for the most inspiring fourth place finish in the history of baseball.

In our breathless media age, when the Bucs came out after the All-Star break and won four of six from the Astros and Reds, the story quickly changed to the Pirates being the story of the century. On July 15, after Jeff Karstens needed only eighty-three pitches to shut out the Astros in Houston, the Pittsburgh Pirates were in first place on the National League Central Division.

The highlight of this stretch, fittingly, in this, the Year of the Rain Delay, was a scene right out of *The Natural*. After one rain delay, they decided to start the opening game of a series with the Reds despite ominous black clouds above us and lightning in the distance. Charlie Morton quickly loaded the bases with two outs in the first. As Morton delivered a two-strike pitch against a coal black sky, there was a bolt of lightning in right center field, followed *much* too quickly by a roll of thunder. If it really had been *The Natural*, it would have been strike three. Instead it was ball one and some of the Reds were rushing for the dugout even before the umpire called it.

When they picked it up a couple hours later, rookie shortstop Chase d'Arnaud, still filling in for the Fantastic Ronny C, made two plays that led to a 2-0 victory that ended shortly after midnight. When play finally resumed, the bases still were loaded for the Reds in the first. Miguel Cairo hit a shot up the middle that looked like it would unravel Charlie Morton. d'Arnaud somehow got behind second and made a backhand flip to Neil Walker just in time to end the inning. A couple innings later, d'Arnaud took an extra base and a knee to his head when he slid into third. This turned a groundout and a fly-out into the only two runs of the game.

Plays like that and an equally stirring 1-0 shutout by James McDonald and the bullpen the next night led the national media to turn their full attention to the Bucs. For the first time in memory, the Bucs even were slotted in for a couple national television appearances. The Pittsburgh Pirates finally mattered.

Then Albert Pujols and the St. Louis Cardinals came to town. As Pujols and his henchmen Lance Berkman and Matt Holliday bombed away in 6-4 and 9-1 clubbings, and showed the baseball world and the Pirates exactly the kind of line-up they did not have, the bandwagon emptied as quickly as it had filled. The Bucs did manage to avoid a sweep on Sunday in the Pirate small-ball way. Xavier Paul got an infield hit in the tenth, stole second, went to third on the catcher's wild throw, and came home on a short sacrifice fly by d'Arnaud.

It was an important win and it was the new Pirate baseball but clearly it would not be enough. You can only win so many games like that. The Pirates had gone another week without a home run. Plus, rookie outfielder Alex Presley, who had given them a huge lift, already had gone on the disabled list with d'Arnaud soon to follow.

There was only a week to go until the trade deadline. The Pirates had to get a hitter.

CHAPTER SEVEN:

DO-OVER

There was one other possibility.

****

In the movie *City Slickers*, a favorite of mine, an attractive young woman, played by Helen Slater, laments that the three city slicker childhood friends, played by Billy Crystal, Daniel Stern and the late Bruno Kirby, know nothing about relationships but they know who played third base for the 1960 Pirates. To which they reply, in unison, "Don Hoak!"

Don Hoak was an ex-Marine and when he came over from the Reds in 1959 he brought toughness and competitiveness to a team that was trying to learn how to fight its way out of the bottom of the National League, as it finally would do in 1960. Hoak was an important player on that 1960 Pirate team and it was altogether fitting, especially for me, that he was the player they used in *City Slickers* to show what little boys hang onto for the rest of their lives.

In 1965, when I was eight years old, my parents were selling our house in the suburbs and we were moving to the city. Many people came to look at it. I happened to be home one afternoon when a tall man with a short haircut and a woman came to our door. I did not really notice the woman even though she was beautiful and, it turned out, a renowned actress and singer of the day named Jill Corey. But I sure as heck knew who her husband was. I tugged on my mother's arm and whispered urgently and a little too loudly: "Don Hoak!"

****

There is another scene in *City Slickers* that might be about the third baseman for the Pittsburgh Pirates. Curly is dead and one of his underlings, charged with helping the vacationing city folk bring in the herd, instead is mean drunk and threatening to shoot Norman, the calf that Billy Crystal delivered from Norman's dying mother, and then slugs Crystal too.

Fueled by his rage at the people who have bullied him, including the father-in-law for whom he worked and the wife on whom he has cheated, Daniel Stern saves the day, turning the gun on the drunken cowhands who flee and are never seen again. Back in the tent, Stern breaks down. He is almost forty years old, he has committed adultery and lost his job, and he thinks he never will see his kids again.

To console him, Crystal and Kirby remind him of how they would play ball when they were kids. When they hit a ball into a tree, they would yell "do-over." His life, they explained, was a do-over.

****

In the last four months of 2010, Pedro Alvarez hit sixteen home runs and drove in sixty-four runs.

In nearly four months of 2011, Pedro Alvarez hit two home runs and drove in ten.

He was placed on the disabled list in May with a pulled quad muscle. As weeks turned into months, it became clear that there was more to it than that. If there was any doubt, it went away when Alvarez was optioned to the minor leagues.

All of this was deeply discouraging for Pirate fans and had to be even more so for Alvarez. So much of the team they were trying to build depended on having at least one guy they could count on to hit the ball out of the park. Pedro Alvarez was supposed to be that guy. If Pedro Alvarez failed, it would affect them for years.

They wanted to give him more time to work things out. Then Alex Presley got hurt and an offense that had struggled all season was even worse. The Pirates were in the heart of the schedule and, against all odds, they were in the race. They had no choice. After nearly two months, Pedro Alvarez was coming back.

Pedro Alvarez was about to get his do-over. He appears to be an amiable young man. Like Daniel Stern, he needs to learn how to fight back, to find the Don Hoak inside him. How it goes could decide the season.

CHAPTER EIGHT:

THE TIES THAT BIND

On vacation in Swampscott, Massachusetts. In a tiny hotel room, following on Gamecast, blackberry dying, laptop almost out too. It is 1:30 am on July 27. Six hours ago, when it started, the Pittsburgh Pirates were in first place:

Andee, awakened from her sleep as I go to plug the laptop into an outlet in the bathroom: This is starting to get out of hand.

Me: That may be but I just got emails from both of your daughters.

Rachel, College Station, Texas: Good thing this game wasn't being played in Pittsburgh–I don't think you'd ever be able to convince Mom to go to another one…Top of the eighteenth as I write....

Lauren, Chicago, Illinois: still up watching this damn game

Me: Damn.

Atlanta 4 Pittsburgh 3.

Nineteen innings.

On a safe call at home, after six hours and thirty-nine minutes, on a guy who was out by twelve feet, about which major league baseball apologized and an ESPN blog declared: "We have a new worst call ever."

Lauren: i curse them when i stay up to watch a bucco-brave game.

CHAPTER NINE:

DEADLINE

July ended with a thud, a weekend sweep by the Phillies in Philadelphia. It looked like the Pirates would salvage the final game, as they had the preceding Sunday against the Cardinals, until Raul Ibanez erased a 5-3 Pirate lead in the eighth with his second homer of the game and then won it with a double in the tenth.

It was a painful end to a painful week. The Phillies may be the best team in baseball and the grueling four-game, forty-seven-inning split in Atlanta could not have helped. As several of the blogs pointed out, the Pirates lost three games in extra innings this week and Joel Hanrahan did not pitch in any of them.

By the end of July, the Bucs had fallen four and a half games behind the Brewers and two and a half games behind the Cards. The sad and unavoidable fact was that the Brewers and the Cardinals were much better teams than the Pirates. The key was to ignore this fact, as the Bucs had done for four months now.

It would not be easy. If the Pirates were not quite dog tired, they looked like they would be soon. Six players were hitting below .200 since the All-Star break. As feared, the starting pitchers were becoming victims of their own success, with almost all of them soon headed for the most innings they had ever pitched. Charlie Morton in particular was starting to falter.

They would begin August with seven games at PNC Park. It would be good to be home.

It would be even better to get some reinforcements. As rarely happens, the Pirates were buyers at the trade deadline. Ryan Ludwick had been an All-Star for the St. Louis Cardinals and less so since for the San Diego Padres. He was hitting .238 and even worse than that in July. Still, Ludwick had more homers than any Pirate except Andrew McCutchen and had driven in as many runs through July as McCutchen and Walker. With Tabata weeks from returning and Presley still on the disabled list, it was worth a chance.

If Ryan Ludwick engendered hope, there was genuine enthusiasm for Derrek Lee. D-Lee once had been a great player, a huge, power-hitting first baseman who also was a graceful fielder. Derrek Lee was not the player he once was but he still was a dangerous hitter. He also was hot and his reputation was that he played his best baseball in the second half. If a pennant race could bring back the young Derrek Lee for a couple months it would make a tremendous difference in a shaky batting order.

This meant the end of the road for Lyle Overbay. The Pirates paid over five million dollars to Lyle Overbay to stabilize first base for them in 2011. It was a mistake. Players get old and sometimes they get old very quickly. In Lyle Overbay, the Pirates got an old player. It was painful to watch. Give Lyle Overbay this, though. On July 31, after he knew that the Pirates had traded for Derrek Lee to take his job, Lyle Overbay went out and hit a home run to give the Pirates a late-inning lead in an important game against the best team in the National League. As Andee pointed out, watching Overbay round the bases, "it says something about the man."

Lyle Overbay had carried himself like a pro. As Clint Hurdle said, though, this was not a try-it league. This was a do-it league. For all of their shocking success, and all they had endured, if the Pittsburgh Pirates wanted to make 2011 a season truly to remember, it was time to do it.

August:

CHAPTER ONE:
IMPLOSION

And then the roof fell in.

After the brutal road trip to Atlanta and Philadelphia, the Pirates headed home to get healthy against two of the weakest teams in the National League, the Chicago Cubs and the San Diego Padres. Seven days later, they had a ten-game losing streak and found themselves ten games out of first place in the Central Division.

It was a team effort. Here is a quick rundown. In five of the ten games, the starting pitcher was shelled and gave the Pirates little chance to win. In two games, the bullpen blew a two-run lead in the eighth inning, and, in two others, they turned a close game into a rout. The defense did not help. The hitting actually was pretty good. The Pirates scored almost four runs a game, which is a lot for them. But not late in games when it mattered most and, when Charlie Morton threw seven courageous shutout innings at the Cubs, they didn't score any at all in a 1-0 loss. There also were some strategy decisions that didn't work. Their nuclear weapon, Joel Hanrahan, remained in the silo at every meaningful juncture. The San Diego series was a disaster, as the weak-hitting Padres lit up the Pirates for thirty-five runs in three games.

For four months, the Pirates had been playing their hearts out and playing better, maybe a lot better, than they really were. This was both admirable and very hard to sustain.

There also is little question when the karma broke. It was the nineteen-inning loss to the Braves with its outrageous ending. But if it hadn't been that, it would have been something else. That loss would not have sent the Phillies into a tailspin. The Phillies are too good for that. The Pirates aren't. It did not take much to tip them over.

I will leave any bashing to others. There is a reason that no culprits are mentioned above. It has been an inspiring summer, far more than I could have hoped when I made my kamikaze commitment last fall to attend 40 Pirate games this season.

Whatever happens now, I am grateful to the Pittsburgh Pirates for the summer of 2011.

CHAPTER TWO:

TELSTAR

If the Bucs were going to dig themselves out of this mess, they would need to start in San Francisco against the World Champion Giants. In the baseball I grew up with, it would be the first stop on a "West Coast swing." It would not be a three-game series followed by a flight to Milwaukee. It would not be the place where a sick team would go to get well. And, most of all, it would not be on television.

By the late 1990s, almost any sporting event that was important to somebody was on television. A few years ago, they extended this to your computer and, more recently, to your phone. Someday, they will cut out all of the middlemen and send the broadcast via satellite directly to your brain.

****

In October 1962, I sprawled on the floor of my parents' bedroom late in the afternoon to watch the San Francisco Giants play the Los Angeles Dodgers for the National League pennant. It was a black and white television, of course, the same television where, later that month, we would watch Adlai Stevenson's speech at the United Nations in the Cuban Missile Crisis.

This was a very big deal. In 1962, a broadcast from the West Coast might as well have been from the moon. In fact, I saw a broadcast from the moon before I remember seeing another baseball game broadcast from the West Coast.

It was the 165th game of the season and it was a classic. The Giants and Dodgers, both only a few years removed from New York, had battled furiously down the stretch at a time when there were no divisions, no wild card teams and no playoff unless there was a tie. There was a tie in 1962; the Dodgers and the Giants each won a hundred and one games and then they split the first two games of a three-game playoff.

Just as in the last playoff between these same two teams, in 1951, when they were the Brooklyn Dodgers and the New York Giants, it looked like the Dodgers had them. On the strength of the last three of Maury Wills' 104 stolen bases in 1962 and the last two of Tommy Davis' 153 RBIs, the Dodgers took a 4-2 lead into the ninth inning in Los Angeles of the deciding game. But, also as in 1951, the Dodgers weren't home free.

The Giants would bring three Hall of Famers to the plate in the top of the ninth. Two of them were kids, Willie McCovey and Orlando Cepeda. The third one was in his prime, which I was too young to appreciate. I saw him later, when he was merely great and later still, as a New York Met in the 1973 World Series, when he was tragic. In his prime, though, and according to a very reliable source—my father, who has seen pretty much all of them—Willie Mays was the greatest baseball player who ever played.

When the Giants came back in the ninth, Willie Mays was right in the middle of it as he almost always was. That much I could have guessed, even though I had not recalled the details. Mays' single made it 4-3 and the Giants were in business. Cepeda drove in the tying run, and the G-Men went on to break the hearts of Dodger fans, just as they had on Bobby Thompson's legendary 1951 homer, The Shot Heard 'Round the World, eleven years earlier to the day.

****

I did not see the Pirates on television from the West Coast until nearly a decade later. It was their second West Coast swing in 1971. July was turning into August, the sun was shining, the wind was blowing out at Candlestick, and the Buccos were bombing. The Pirates scored twenty-three runs in four games that weekend.

And they lost them all. Like the Pirates, the 1971 Giants were a powerful team. They would meet again, in the playoffs that October. Cepeda was gone but Mays was still a force, twenty years after he stood in the on-deck circle and watched Bobby Thompson's home run. By 1971 Willie McCovey was a monster. They were joined by an incredibly gifted young outfielder named Bobby Bonds who, at the much-too-fleeting height of his game, may have been even more talented than his son, and a gigantic, free-swinging rookie first baseman named Dave Kingman who that weekend would hit the first of his 442 home runs, a grand slam in a 15-11 Giant win, along with the first of his 1816 strikeouts.

The Pirates went into that road trip 63-34. They came home 67-41. Even the best teams rarely did much on the West Coast.

****

The 2011 Pirates had no choice. They had lost ten games in a row. At least they caught a break. They would miss the Giants' best pitchers, the great artist, Tim Lincecum, and his sidekick, Matt Cain. Besides, it had to end sometime.

It would end on Monday night, on television of course, in the first game of the series, a game that proved, yet again, how little I know about baseball after fifty years of watching it. To the shock of most, after an unmitigated disaster in 2010, Charlie Morton stormed out of the gate in 2011. He was one of the feel-good stories on a feel-good team. By mid-summer, though, Morton's numbers were back to 2010 levels and the Pirates were falling apart. There were questions raised by many about how long the Bucs could hang with Charlie Morton.

Some of those questions were raised by me. After Morton was shelled by the Phillies, I asked my friend Jim how long they could wait before taking Charlie Morton out of the rotation. His answer: "a really long time." Once again, Jim was right. In his next two starts, Ground Chuck was back, with seven shutout innings against the Cubs that should have ended the losing streak and eight shutout innings against the Giants that did end the losing streak.

After a shutout loss, the Bucs came back and took the series thanks to another welcome sight—the return of the Andrew McCutchen who had carried the team through the All-Star break but had slumped since then. McCutchen was on base five straight times, launched a 451-foot home run from his 175-pound body, stole two bases and scored four runs.

If the ship had not been righted, it had been steadied. There was a long, long way to go to get back into contention. The Pirates did not have time for that now anyway. There was a more immediate task at hand. The expression may not have been familiar to people in 1962 or 1971, but it would not have been hard for them to figure out. It was time to man-up and beat the Brewers in Milwaukee.

CHAPTER THREE:

MILLER PARK

Or, they could lose three more and run their record in Milwaukee to 3-36. Except for the end of the first game, the Pirates competed in this series and easily could have won the last two—1-0 and 2-1 losses, despite brilliant pitching performances by Kevin Correia and, once again, Charlie Morton. But then...

I don't even want to talk about it.

CHAPTER FOUR:

KEWANEE

By the second week of August, 1971, my cast was off and my parents took me up to camp. It was a very emotional trip. This was where I was supposed to have been in the summer of 1971. Where I had been every summer since 1966 when, just a few days after I arrived as a nine-year-old, I sliced my leg open on a nail on the Fourth of July and got stitched up in Factoryville, Pennsylvania, a town near the camp with barely over a thousand people.

The doctor's office was just down the street from the statue of the town's most famous native. This tiny little town had produced the first great pitcher of the twentieth century. Christy Mathewson won 373 games for the New York Giants and pitched three straight shutouts in the 1905 World Series. Along with Babe Ruth, Honus Wagner, Ty Cobb and Walter Johnson, he was one of the first five players elected to the Baseball Hall of Fame.

In 1966, we had stormed off the hill down to the lower ball field at Kamp Kewanee to celebrate a Pirate win. Roberto Clemente was at the height of his game. Willie Stargell was just coming into his. The Sheriff, Donn Clendenon. Bonus Baby Beetle Bailey. Maz and Alley turning most of the Bucs'

215 double plays. Harry the Hat Walker teaching Matty Alou to slap it the other way and hit .342. Pags.

The pitching staff would span the generations, Vernon Law and Elroy Face from 1960. The young Steve Blass and Bob Veale from 1971. Woody Fryman, who wandered out of the hills of Kentucky to cause a big stir that summer and, from the Virgin Islands, the Gunner's favorite name of all: Alvin O'Neal McBean.

That Pirate team hung in all summer with the Dodgers and Giants. The kids from Pittsburgh at Kamp Kewanee hung in right with them. If there is nothing like a pennant race, there is *nothing* like your first pennant race.

****

Kamp Kewanee was an unusual camp. It was an almost all Jewish camp. But most of the counselors were from nearby towns and every Sunday morning we would put on our white t-shirts and head down to the lodge for church services. It decidedly was not the co-ed Jewish community center camp at which I would later be a counselor, and where I would meet my wife.

Instead, it was sort of a pre-professional camp. We competed in everything, every day. For most of the day we competed at sports, with each other as well as with other camps and with baseball and basketball teams from nearby towns. We competed to see who had the cleanest fingernails and who could make the neatest beds. Then we competed to see who could put on the best play and who could write the best song. Every year for every age group there would be *College Bowl* and later, my favorite, *Jeopardy.* Future CEOs and their lawyers would need to know something, too. About twenty years ago, I ran into an old friend from camp. We agreed on two things: the values at Kamp Kewanee were way off and we loved that camp.

Every five years or so there is a camp reunion and about 150 people are there. This is no small accomplishment because Kamp Kewanee has not been in existence since 1973. In 2001, I took Lauren with me. She was looking at some colleges in Philadelphia, where the reunion was held. Watching a bunch of forty- to ninety-year-old guys sing old camp songs, she thought we were the strangest people she had ever seen.

Then there was a ceremony and some speakers. One of them was a guy named Jeff who was a couple years ahead of me at camp. Jeff had with him a wooden hatchet that was given to the captains of the Red and Black color war, a huge week-long competition at the end of camp. The results since 1921 were displayed on plaques in the dining hall. I was well aware of what this hatchet was because I am proud to say that I still have one, the red one, from 1972.

Jeff spoke for awhile and it was not clear where he was going or why he had the hatchet with him. But then he asked a man who was about seventy-five years old to come up and join him at the microphone. Jeff explained that his father Cal had been a Red and Black captain in 1942. Cal had wanted to attend the reunion but he got very sick and had passed away that winter. Before he died, he told Jeff that his opposing captain was one of the finest people he ever knew and that, fifty-nine years later, he wanted his friend and fellow 1942 Red and Black captain to have his hatchet.

That was Kamp Kewanee too.

****

When I got to camp in August 1971, there only were a couple weeks to go. I begged my parents and the owners of the camp to let me stay. But my arm was severely atrophied from eight weeks in a cast and they wouldn't chance it. So I came home to the one thing I had in Pittsburgh.

I went down to Three Rivers Stadium by myself to watch one of the pitching match-ups of the year, All-Star Game starter Dock Ellis against that season's Cy Young winner,

Ferguson Jenkins, who would win twenty-four games in 1971. Bob Prince always called him Ferguson Jenkins and His Orchestra. I'm sure there was a reason for that—or maybe not.

Fergie Jenkins was the rare Hall of Fame player acquired by trade. He had been traded by the Phillies early in the 1966 season along with two other minor players for a couple of once prominent but over the hill pitchers. It is not mentioned with the Lou Brock for Ernie Broglio trade, which remains the poster child for the genre, but, seven twenty-game winning seasons later, the Jenkins trade was every bit the heist.

For the Bucs, Dock Ellis was in his own movie, as he always was. The Doctor was starting to fade after carrying the staff for the first half of his career year. He would come up lame in the first game of the World Series and be done for the year. But in August he still had a few good battles left in him and one of them was against Ferguson Jenkins and His Orchestra.

For a pitchers' duel like this, the place to be was behind home plate. Alas, I was down the right field line. Down 1-0, Ellis held the fort until the Pirates scored two in the fifth, taking the lead on Clemente's double to left. Ellis outlasted Jenkins, who left for a pinch hitter in the eighth, and then the Cubs tied it in the top of the ninth. But Ellis worked out of it and pitched the full nine innings. That was all he needed when, after a double by Vic Davalillo and walks to Clemente and Stargell, Richie Hebner singled off Phil “the Vulture” Regan towards me in right to win it for the Bucs.

The Pirates of 1971 were not trying to find a way to break .500 for the first time in nineteen years. They were 71-46. They plugged Clemente and Stargell into the three and four spots every night and surrounded them with some terrific young hitters. They had enough pitching and defense and they were taking control of the National League East.

CHAPTER FIVE:

SENIOR DAY

The 2011 Pirates had trimmed their sails. The big homestand against the Cardinals, Reds and Brewers didn't look so big anymore. It still was special in one way. It was a chance to go to a baseball game with my son.

When David was little, we went to games all the time, games we watched, games David played. He was a better ballplayer than his dad even if his real game was golf, which he got from his mother's side. We were as close as a father and son could be, probably too close. He needed to break away and become his own person—and he did. There have been many times when our relationship was like the rest of that scene from *City Slickers*, when Daniel Stern explains to Helen Slater that it may be childish to remember Don Hoak, but that there were times in his life that the only thing he and his dad could talk about was baseball.

As David became his own person, he also became his own man, with an adventurous spirit that will serve him well and that he did not get from me. When he was young, a friend of mine once commented about David at a picnic: "Look, he is just like his dad. He checks everything out to make sure it's OK and then he joins in."

Somewhere along the road, that went away. A few years ago, when he was a student at the University of Wisconsin, David did a semester abroad, in Ghana, with a guest family he came to love, in a house without running water. Dropping him at the airport in Philadelphia, Andee and I were ready for an anxious goodbye as we sent our youngest child halfway around the world to a place we knew nothing about. Instead, it was a quick hug and he never looked back, just a kid in shorts in the dead of winter (some things never change), a young man now, with a backpack loaded down with a copy of *War and Peace* and ready to take on the world.

David is a gifted writer, as anyone who has read his letters from Ghana knows. In another place and time, I would have asked him to write this with me. He would have made this book better. But what David writes about is usually much weightier and, when it isn't, I have come to understand, it still is his.

So I didn't ask him and we would not do this together. But we would go to a game.

Fittingly, the star of the homestand opening victory over the Cardinals was Ryan Doumit, returned from his broken ankle. The last game that just David and I had gone to together was on David's seventeenth birthday, in 2005, when Ryan Doumit was a rookie. This was the game where the young Doumit repeatedly threatened to and finally succeeded in throwing the ball over the third baseman's head after a strikeout. It was a game David and I both remember well.

Now Ryan Doumit is thirty years old and finishing what likely will be his seventh and last summer in Pittsburgh. Doumit is not that much older than David. But as David is just taking the first steps toward his life's work, whatever that turns out to be, Ryan Doumit is close to the end of his. No matter how much money they make, the short working life of an athlete must be a frightening thing.

I heard an interview with Doumit earlier this year. In this interview, he said that he feels that he is a better player than people have seen and that he only has a few more years to show it. It was thoughtful and mature and much different than the Ryan Doumit of the past seven years.

With that in mind, and with genuine enthusiasm, we cheered Ryan Doumit as he went four for four and broke open the game with a three-run homer or, as Earl Weaver used to call it, the best play in baseball. Then Jose Veras locked it down when he froze Albert Pujols, greatest hitter of the generation, on a strike three curve.

For the Pirates, it was a win they desperately needed. For me, it was my thirtieth game of the season. I was 12-18. But, together, David and I were undefeated.

CHAPTER SIX:
THE BUSINESS OF HOPE

The Pittsburgh Pirates are in the business of hope. For a generation they have been in the business of false hope. There is a chance that they are in the business of false hope now. But even as the season that had been so promising was turning into a long march to the end, the Pirates did two smart things that were good news for a team that desperately needed some.

The baseball draft has been a big part of the failure of the past eighteen years. One way or another, the Pirates almost always have ended up a step behind. For many years, the Pirates were accused, fairly or not, of passing over better players to draft lesser players who would be cheaper to sign. That stopped when they drafted Pedro Alvarez. Whether or not they are picking the right players, at least now there is no dispute that they are trying.

This year, the Pirates had the first pick of the draft, thanks to their 105 losses in 2010. They selected a pitcher from UCLA named Gerrit Cole and signed him for $8 million. This was important but not surprising. The surprise was in the next round. With the sixty-first pick, the Pirates drafted a 6-5, switch-hitting high school outfielder from Texas named

Josh Bell whom the Pirates had rated the sixth best player in the draft and who most teams had in the top fifteen. The reason Josh Bell was available was that he had written a letter to every team telling them not to draft him because he was going to the University of Texas. In the second round, the Pirates took a chance and then, on the last day, August 15, and to the shock of teams all over baseball, they signed him. People in baseball even criticized the Pirates for spending too much money to do it, which was ironic to say the least.

Will anyone ever hear of Josh Bell again? Who knows? But it was the kind of move the Pirates never used to make, the kind of move you make when you know what you're doing. Then, a week later, the Pirates did something even better. They signed Jose Tabata to a long-term contract at a reasonable price, one that could keep him with the Pirates through 2019. There was talk that they were making progress on a deal with Neil Walker, too. The big fish, Andrew McCutchen, was going to be harder but even there they had a chance.

The Pirates also received some unexpected help from a misbegotten draft gone by. In 2006, the Pirates passed over Tim Lincecum to draft Brad Lincoln. While Lincecum already had won two Cy Young awards and a World Series on his way to the Hall of Fame, Brad Lincoln was stuck pitching in Triple A.

Five years later, after yet another season in the minors, the Pirates gave Brad Lincoln a chance. He had been battered around when they brought him up in 2010. He had done better in a double-header call-up in Washington this past June. Now he was up again in late August. If this was not his last chance, he would not have many more.

One of the reasons the Pirates drafted Brad Lincoln way back when is that he is a battler. In six days in late August, Lincoln battled two former Cy Young winners, Zach Greinke of the Brewers and Chris Carpenter of the Cardinals, and he outpitched both of them. After giving up two in the first to the Brewers, Brad Lincoln pitched eleven straight shutout innings against two of the best hitting teams in baseball. Brad Lincoln was back in the big leagues and the Pittsburgh Pirates were back in the business of hope.

CHAPTER SEVEN:

RECIPE FOR DISASTER

1. Get a lead.
2. Stop hitting.
3. Pull the starting pitcher a little too late.
4. Watch the bullpen collapse.
5. Lose.

The Pirates did that five times in six games at the end of August. Jeff Karstens, so brilliant in June and July, was worn down and close to being shut down. Maholm and Correia already were gone for the season with injuries. A month earlier, the Pirates had considered going to a six-man rotation to save pitchers who had been pitching far more innings than they had in the past. Looking back, that would have been a very good idea.

Hope can only take you so far. At the end of August, the Pirates were 62-74. It was breathtaking how quickly this had happened. On July 25, the Pirates were in first place. On August 31, thirty-seven days later, they were eighteen and a half games back. They were completely out of gas. And they still had a month to play.

SEPTEMBER:

CHAPTER ONE:

THE LONG WALK HOME

I was a Bear.

In the 14th Ward Little League that was a good thing to be. Then as now, team stacking was the order of the day in the 14th Ward and in the late 1960s nobody did it better than the Bears. Unless it was the Tartans.

It was a good league, especially when you included the tougher kids from the Frick Park side. As for me, I was pretty good for Little League, but that was it. I loved to play, but the better athletes already were starting to catch and pass me.

My parents came to as many games as they could. They made it to almost all of them. Once in a while, when they couldn't make it, I would walk home. It was a long walk, almost two miles, in my Footer's Cleaners Bears uniform and carrying my baseball glove, the Wilson A2002 for lefties. By the time I got home, I was beat, it was nearly dark, and I had almost forgotten how much fun I'd just had.

The summer of 2011 had been better than you could imagine, better than anyone ever could have hoped. But, in September, the Pittsburgh Pirates were taking that long walk home.

CHAPTER TWO:

ROCK BOTTOM

After being swept by the Houston Astros, the worst team in baseball, the Pirates came home on September 1 for a late afternoon make-up game against the Dodgers in front of Andee and me and a couple thousand of our closest friends. It featured one of the lowest points of the season, the return of the full 2010 feeling and, for a painful moment, the old Ryan Doumit.

Brad Lincoln gave up three in the first and then rallied through five scoreless innings as Pirate hitters were making soft-tossing lefty Dana Eveland—shelled and released as a Pirate in 2010—look like Tommy John, just as my friend Jim had assured us he would. Jim is embittered these days; his heart has been broken by the Pirates one too many times.

I am more patient. I would like to think it is because I take the long view. I know it is because I have not loved as hard or as long. But I have loved enough. If I am more patient, there is a limit.

In the seventh inning, with runners on first and third, Ryan Doumit gave up a passed ball. Then he did not make a play at home as the runner scored from third. Then he stood there holding the ball as the runner on first went all the way to third.

Shortly after that, in the eighth inning, we did something we had not done in thirty-six games. Something we almost never do at any sporting event. We left.

CHAPTER THREE:
FAITH

The Future

Alex Presley is 5-9 on a good day and he looks like he is twelve years old. A mid-round pick out of the University of Mississippi in 2007, Alex Presley had a nondescript minor league career until he unexpectedly blossomed as a hitter in 2010. This earned him a September 2010 call-up for good behavior, not because he was viewed as an important part of the future.

David and I liked him, though; we liked his swing and we liked his speed. We were surprised when he did not make the team coming out of spring training. But Presley didn't sulk. He went back to AAA and tore the cover off the ball until they had to bring him back. Then he did the same thing in Pittsburgh. He was a big reason for what happened in July. After he was called-up, Alex Presley hit .333 and the Pirates played .600 baseball. Then he got hurt and, for that reason and others, the Pirates fell apart.

By the time Presley came back in late August, the pennant race was over. But there still was time to see if Alex Presley was a player they could win with someday. The early returns were encouraging. In the first four games in September, Presley had ten hits and continued to show surprising pop with a double, two triples and a home run.

Alex Presley may look like a batboy but he can hit. He has a smooth and quick left-handed stroke and he hits to all fields. It is beautiful to watch. More than anything, he is a throwback. He looks like he should be wearing a baggy flannel uniform.

Young hitters come and go. They get figured out. Alex Presley isn't going anywhere.

The Past

The Pirates were following the script. Get a lead, stop hitting, starter falters, bullpen collapses. With the game interrupted by a rain delay in Chicago, we headed out for the opening of the Pitt football season. We thought the Pirate game would be rained out as a 5-3 loss. But I checked the blackberry at Heinz Field and the game was back on. Down two in the ninth against Cubs closer Carlos Marmol, this seemed a formality.

Still, I gave updates to my father and my Uncle Stanley. Time marches on. They had gone to games in the 1930s, before the first baseball game shown on television. Now they were tracking one on a blackberry. Marmol was unsteady. After a single by Xavier Paul, walks to Tabata and McCutchen loaded the bases with two out. A single would tie the game. It was time for the National Anthem. I put the blackberry away.

When the anthem ended, I hit refresh and did a double take. The blackberry said the score was 7-5. Derrek Lee had hit a grand slam off Carlos Marmol with two outs in the top of the ninth. It was Lee's first game back, a month after Marmol had hit him with a pitch and broken his hand. Two days later, Lee broke up another game with an eighth inning home run off Astros closer Wilton Lopez. He hit both of them in a driving rain.

The Pirates lost a lot when Derrek Lee broke his hand. They lost power. They lost defense. Most of all they lost *gravitas*. The line-up felt different when Derrek Lee was in it, almost the way it used to feel when they had Willie Stargell. It would have been nice to have seen Derrek Lee in the middle of that line-up during a pennant race. That didn't happen. Now, we would just have to watch him show a bunch of young kids how a real pro plays baseball.

CHAPTER FOUR:

EMANCIPATION

No discussion of the 1971 Pittsburgh Pirates would be complete without this:

Rennie Stennett, 2B
Gene Clines, CF
Roberto Clemente, RF
Willie Stargell, LF
Manny Sanguillen, C
Dave Cash, 3B
Al Oliver, 1B
Jackie Hernandez, SS
Dock Ellis, P

It has been the subject of countless articles and even a book. This was the Pirates starting line-up on September 1, 1971. Twenty-four years after Jackie Robinson, it is believed to have been the first non-white line-up in the history of baseball. Only six of them were batting over .300.

CHAPTER FIVE:

THE HOME STRETCH

Not surprisingly, that line-up pounded the Phillies 10-7. Dock Ellis was knocked out in the second. No matter. Six Pirate hitters had two hits and Sangy of all people hit one out of the park. The following Saturday I wandered down to Three Rivers by myself to watch the Pirates survive an afternoon of rain and six—count 'em, six—errors to outlast the Expos. The '71 Bucs were capable of that every once in a while, too.

This is the last game I remember until the playoffs. After that, it was back to the tenth grade. Not to worry. The Bucs had the National League East in hand. The Cardinals were hanging around, thanks largely to a career year by Joe Torre who would win the National League MVP over Willie Stargell. With due and genuine respect for Torre's .363 average, this was a travesty and not one of baseball's proudest moments.

The Pirates would clinch a tie on September 18, their 93rd win, a two-hit shutout by Steve Blass. It took all of one hour and forty-two minutes, roughly the amount of time players spend in a game these days adjusting their batting gloves, as they now do after nearly every pitch.

The Bucs of 1971 had it under control. They were looking ahead to the playoffs and the World Series and so were we. This will give me time to get to a couple things that have been on my mind all summer and a lot longer than that.

CHAPTER SIX:

THE PARK NEAR OUR HOUSE

In 1983, Andee was expecting our first child and we were looking for a home to raise our family. We knew that someday we wanted to live in the city, where we both had grown up and gone to high school. For now, we couldn't afford that and, besides, I had lived in one of the eastern suburbs, Churchill, as a small child, during one of the happiest times of my life.

We looked in lots of places. One sunny afternoon, we were driving down a series of winding hills in an area not far from Churchill. As we went down one more hill, I told Andee we should keep going, that I knew this place. That if you just keep going down, you will hit a baseball field.

I only had been there one time. It was in 1962. Good friends of my parents knew that I liked baseball. One night they took me to watch their son's Little League game. I piled into the back seat of their station wagon with his younger sister, who was about my age. Ten years later, when we all had moved into the city, most of my friends in high school would have killed to have been in the back seat of a station wagon with her, but that's a whole other story.

In 1962, in Pittsburgh and everywhere else, suburban communities were springing to life. Most of the people who lived in them were the young families who had won the war. They were reaping the rewards of their sacrifice and of the staggering material progress of the post-war world. In the eyes of a five-year-old, and even looking back on it now, it was a time of great optimism.

That optimism was reflected in the Blackridge Little League that night in 1962. There were kids and young parents everywhere. There was a concession stand. I would not go to a Pirate game until the following spring. As far as I was concerned, this was the big leagues. One of the older kids hit one into the woods in left. To me, he was Willie Mays and I can still see the ball rising into those trees. Not long ago, I dreamed that I did it myself.

When Andee and I found the Blackridge Little League field in 1983, the backstop was not in good shape and it did not look like anyone played there any more. But except for that, the park was thoughtfully maintained. There still was a real community spirit in Blackridge even if it was different from the *Camelot* optimism I remember from that night in 1962.

We moved into a little house about half a mile up the hill. The Little League was gone but that park became an important part of our lives. We all called it "The Park Near Our House." We pitched to the kids there but mostly they played on the swings and the see-saw and the jungle gym in deep right center field. Andee would sing to them and they would laugh and sing to her and on the see-saw we all would sing "The Famous Duke of York." Every 4th of July all the parents in the neighborhood would decorate their kids' bikes and everyone would roll down the hill for a parade to the park.

Sometimes dreams come true. A few years ago, fifteen years after we moved from Blackridge into the city, Lauren, Rachel and David said they had a surprise for us. It was a beautiful night in August. They took us in one car and their grandparents in another. Soon we were in our old neighborhood. We started going down the hill. If there could be one perfect way to spend our twenty-fifth anniversary it would be a picnic dinner arranged by our children and it would be at The Park Near Our House. If my parents' friends had not taken me to a Little League game in 1962, none of it might ever have happened.

CHAPTER SEVEN:

1962

It is a mystery. My mother assures me she never would have thrown them out. I believe her.

On April 28, 1966, our family moved into the city, to my grandparents' house, the house where my mother grew up. With me on this six-mile journey were a few hundred football cards, all of which I still have to this day. Not with me were my baseball cards, thousands of them. It only bothers me when I think about it.

****

It was the most inspired baby gift we ever received. A full set of 1988 baseball cards. For more than ten years after that, Andee and I would faithfully order a set of baseball cards and hide them away. The plan was to give all of them to David for his bar mitzvah.

The problem is that by the time you are thirteen years old you don't care about baseball cards anymore. Not even me. You might come back to them later in life, for a different reason, but you don't care about them when you are thirteen.

We didn't give these cards to David. To this day, he has no idea that we did this. But someday, when David has a child...

****

In the early 1960s, once or twice a summer, my parents would let me walk up to Fierst's, the gas station by the new Churchill high school, and buy a *box* of baseball cards. Twenty packs. For a dollar. I would open all of them right there, a stick of gum in every pack. I don't think I ever got all twenty sticks in my mouth at once, but I was close. My dentist says that I have the thickest file of any patient he has. It was honestly earned.

Every little boy has a favorite baseball card year. Mine was 1962. When our kids were little we used to take them to baseball card shows. They each had their own collections. Once in a while, one of the booths would have unopened packs of old baseball cards, sometimes from as far back as the 1960s. The older the packs the more they would cost. You never knew when you might find a Mickey Mantle or a Warren Spahn, although I always suspected that anything like that had been surgically removed.

I never bought one from the 1960s. They were about $100. There were tuitions down the road and a mortgage to consider. More than anything, I never saw a pack from 1962. For that I would have paid almost any price.

You can buy baseball cards from 1962 at card shows or, these days, online I assume. I have never tried. It's not the same. An unopened pack is as close as you can get. Except for one thing. It came from the most unexpected source at an even more unexpected time.

CHAPTER EIGHT:

BILL

I had a brother.

In the summer of 1971, I stayed in his room. It had the air conditioner and I was in a cast. He was gone for a lot of it. I think he left to start college as a late entry into the freshman class at the University of Colorado. A gifted classical pianist who had practiced four hours a day since he was four years old, he had chucked it all and he never really went back. Colorado had not been the plan, but that's where he was.

He had a short wave radio I used all that summer. I would listen to the late games when the Pirates were on the West Coast, to breaking news of the *Pentagon Papers* and Nixon's wage-price freeze, and, endlessly, to the Top 40 songs of the summer of 1971. "Smiling Faces." "It's Too Late Baby." "Draggin' the Line." "That's the Way I Always Heard It Should Be." "Do You Know What I Mean?"

Bill used it to listen to radio stations all over the world. He spoke about seven languages. He would collect "QSL cards" from these stations. One year, he and I listened to New Year's in about five different time zones.

There was a poster in his room. "Old Soldiers Never Die. Young Ones Do." It was 1971. He was eighteen years old. On top of everything else, the specter of Viet Nam hung over him. He never went, but two years later he was in training in a tank in the Israeli Army just after the Yom Kippur War. It was a job to which he was singularly unsuited, but he did it.

My brother had a deep sense of what was important and he rose to the biggest occasions. When Andee and I were married, as the best man, he gave a toast that I will never forget about what it meant to have a Jewish wedding. Shortly before he died, he played the piano and sang at our sister's wedding. When Lauren was born, he snuck a tape recorder into the hospital to record her cries on her first day on this earth.

Bill traced the history of our family back for centuries. This was a truly remarkable undertaking, the accomplishment of a lifetime, and he knew it. Recently, and to his great credit, David has helped my mother supplement and digitize this effort. There are things that I could add. The Mother's Day cake that Bill and I tried to ride home on our bicycles in 1966; the second one we bought because he was crushed when the first one fell. Running together in Schenley Park in 1974 when he was getting ready to go back to the Israeli Army and I was heading to college. In the early 1980s, when he would show up at our apartment at 11:30 at night to watch *Fridays* and *SCTV* with Andee and me. The list of restaurants we went to when he got sick, when that was the last thing he could really enjoy. Lauren's memory of her Uncle Bill in her bat mitzvah speech.

There are other things that I would not include. They are between us. And there is one thing that is just for me. We found it in the early 1990s, a year or so after he died. It was a letter from Kamp Kewanee, where Bill had gone for many years before I did. The letter was postmarked July 2, 1962. My brother sent it to our house on Marbury Road at "Pittsburgh 21, Pa." which is how you used to do it, and it was to me:

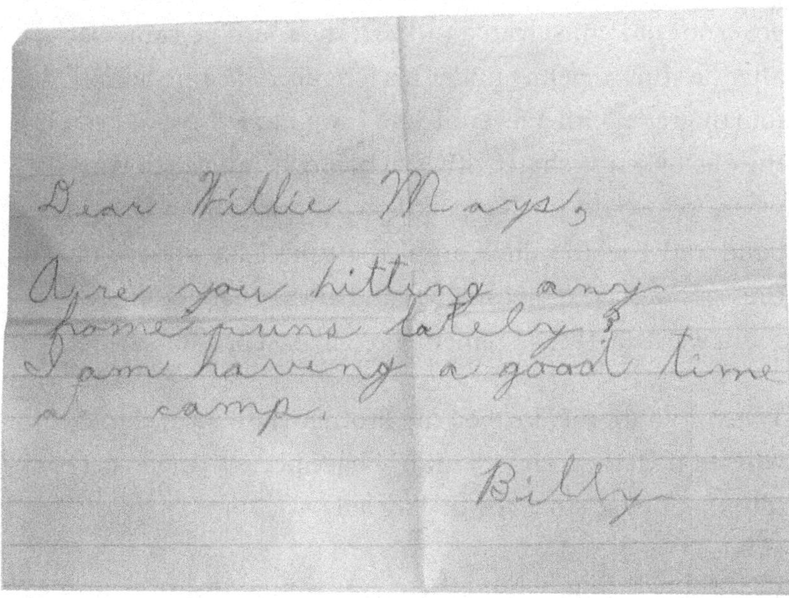
Dear Willie Mays,
Are you hitting any home runs lately?
I am having a good time at camp.
Billy

Inside the letter were baseball cards from 1962, including Bill Mazeroski. My brother was an artist in the truest sense. In time, that made it hard, hard for us, harder for him. But in 1962, when he was nine years old, he was just a happy kid sending home some baseball cards to his little brother.

When our own kids were little and we lived in Blackridge, we walked a mile or two over to Marbury Road to see some friends, the same friends who gave David the set of baseball cards as a baby gift. On the way, we passed the house where I grew up. The family who lived there was outside. I explained that I had lived there over twenty years earlier and asked if I could come in. There was still the same blue carpet in my brother's room in the basement, the room he, Peggy and I paraded around in when William Scranton was elected governor of Pennsylvania in 1962, the room he came back to after he stuck a penny under his tongue and came home from fourth grade with a fever of 106. I went to my room upstairs, the one I used to share with him before he moved downstairs, where he would hit the paddle with the ball on the rubber band and I would duck, until the time I hit my eye on the dresser and had to get stitches and a scar that I still have. My room was exactly as I remembered it, except a lot smaller.

When I got home, I called my brother right away. I told him where I had been. He just said: "I have been trying to get back into that house since the day we left."

I left some things behind there, too.

CHAPTER NINE:

MILESTONE

We have shared everything important since 1978. We would share this.

Truth be told, it was not that important to Andee. "Why are we here again?" But here we were.

I am a very lucky man.

We arrived early. There were two ceremonies. The first was to honor the line-up of September 1, 1971. Roberto Clemente, Willie Stargell and Dock Ellis were gone and Rennie Stennett could not be there. But the rest of them were. Sangy. Dave Cash. Al Oliver. Jackie Hernandez. And Gene Clines. Now he is a smiling sixty-five-year-old man. Back then Bob Prince called him "Little Angry." You would have been too, if you hit .308 in 1971 and .334 in 1972 and couldn't even make the starting line-up.

A quiet moment between a pair of slick-fielding Latin American shortstops forty years apart, Jackie Hernandez and Ronny Cedeño. Then it was on to the main event, Roberto Clemente Day, in Pittsburgh as it was all over baseball. Vera Clemente was there, along with two of their sons, older than Roberto Clemente ever was, but still looking like his children.

On Roberto Clemente Day, every team in baseball nominates a player for exemplary conduct on and off the field. For the Pirates, it was Jeff Karstens. He was an excellent choice. Going into 2011, I am not sure that I ever had given Jeff Karstens five seconds' thought. Now, on this team, for this season, he was my favorite player. The player who got the most out of his ability. The player who competed the hardest. The player who best embodied the spirit of a team that played as hard as it could for as long as it could, which is how I want to remember the 2011 Pittsburgh Pirates.

Those Pirates were gone now and they had been for nearly two months. On this day, it was a close game, a good game. The kind of game they might have won in June and July. Now, even down only a run, it was clear they had no chance.

By the end, there only were a couple thousand people left. We had to stay. This was my fortieth game. I had gone the distance. Andee had made it to half of them. When Jason Jaramillo grounded out to second to end the game, it was another milestone, one that for a long and inspiring time had looked like it would not happen.

"Well, Dear, that makes nineteen years in a row."

It was a sad end to a sweet summer.

CHAPTER TEN:

THAT'S IT, GOOD SEASON

We were back where we started. On the couch with Lauren watching the Pirates. She was in from Chicago with Nick. There were no tears tonight. Only laughter and smiles as the Bucs put it to the Reds on the last Saturday night of the season.

Much had happened since that sad night in the fall of 1992. Lauren's childhood. Her wedding. Nineteen losing seasons in a row.

At a young age, Lauren decided that she was going to make a difference in this world. She already has. Attracted to politics, the hard work side, not the glamorous part, Lauren worked on numerous campaigns, through college and after, for candidates she believed in. All of them lost. Undaunted by this series of brave defeats, she stayed with it. In 2007, Lauren's efforts earned her an early position in the main office in Chicago of an underdog but promising candidate for President of the United States. There, she worked next to a young man named Nick whom Lauren quickly came to learn was a like-minded soul and not long after realized was the love of her life.

Together, Lauren and Nick have accomplished more than most people do in a lifetime. They spent fourteen hours a day for two years, holding each other together in ultra-high pressure jobs in the most important election of our lifetime. I could go on and on but I would just sound like a proud father, which I am. Lauren may have learned from Jim Leyland that night that you don't always win. But she also learned that you never give up. I would like to think she learned some of that from me.

****

As for the Pirates, there will be some who will think they gave up in the last part of this season. It is not what I choose to believe. To me, they just hit the wall. I would much rather see a team that tried and then collapsed than one that accepted its lot in life.

There is, though, the question of whether they are getting anywhere. Anyone who watched them in August and September wouldn't think so. The pitching, so heartening for so long, gave out. There is nothing approaching the kind of ace that the best teams have. Still, Jeff Karstens, Charlie Morton and James McDonald are a start. Kevin Correia will be back, maybe even Paul Maholm, and Brad Lincoln will be ready. I learned this year that you need six or seven. The season is just too long and pitching is an unnatural act. They can build a bullpen around Joel Hanrahan. They need to find a couple more guys who can start.

Andrew McCutchen peered over the edge of greatness in May and June and decided he was not quite ready to take the plunge. Prince Andrew spent the last couple months trying to jack every pitch out of PNC Park. He's only twenty-four and he will get it out of his system. Andrew McCutchen will be fine.

I wish I was as sure about the other biggest piece of the puzzle. Pedro: it is in your hands. Ignore the fifty-year-old men who feel the need to scream at you. Go home, get your head on straight, and start over.

Neil Walker is a proven major league player now. He is not a superstar but he is the kind of player who helps good teams win. Jose Tabata would be too, if he just could stay on the field. It would be good to see what Alex Presley could do for a full year. It would be even better to find a way to talk Derrek Lee into coming back and playing first base.

Someone will need to play shortstop. It would be nice to bring back the Fantastic Ronny C of May and June. After his concussion when we were in Washington on July 1, he was never quite the same. It might even be time to think the unthinkable: bringing back Ryan Doumit to play catcher.

Some of these things won't happen. One way or the other, there will be some new players. They will not be breaking up the '27 Yankees.

Whoever they are, they will have a lot of work to do. Even when they were winning, the 2011 Pirates were a lot better at playing hard than playing smart. They did not run the bases well. They struck out far too much. They gave away too many at-bats, especially late in games. They rarely hit the cut-off man. Bunts were mostly hit or miss. Lots of other things. Hopefully, this is all part of growing up. Hopefully, this just means that there is a lot of room to get better.

I guess you can't write a book about baseball these days without saying something about Moneyball. I believe in it. I know what a walk means. I know what it means to see a lot of pitches. I know there are a hundred ways to help a team win a ballgame, or lose one. Still, I am not a religious adherent. I don't think a bunt is a crime against nature. I believe in Moneyball but I believe in execution even more, and in players learning how to play and reaching their potential.

All that is for next year, and after that. For now, it is done. There would be one more October without baseball in Pittsburgh.

****

There was a time when the Pirates were part of October. Maybe they were playing, maybe they had fallen just short, but they belonged. For a generation, it has felt like the Pirates do not belong. October is the time for the real teams. Teams like the Yankees and the Red Sox, the Phillies and the Cardinals. Teams like the Pittsburgh Pirates of 1971 that stormed past the San Francisco Giants and into the World Series when Bob Robertson hit three homers one afternoon in San Francisco and then Richie Hebner and Al Oliver blasted home runs into a late day sky past my sister and me over the right field fence at Three Rivers Stadium. The team that came back from two games down behind Steve Blass and the great Roberto Clemente to win the World Series against a Baltimore Orioles team that had won sixteen games in a row.

It would mean a lot just to be a part of it again. The Pirates have not been part of October for a long time. They are not part of it now. But, for the first time in a long time, it feels like someday they could be.

In the summer of 2011, the Pittsburgh Pirates brought baseball back to Pittsburgh. They did not get all the way there, but they reminded us of what baseball once had been in Pittsburgh and what it could be again.

In the summer of 2011, the Pittsburgh Pirates also brought baseball back to me. Like the Pirates, I did not reclaim all of my baseball past. But I reclaimed enough. Enough to recapture the summer of 1971 and the summer of 1966 and the summer of 1962. Enough to know this:

Baseball is one of the things you have when you are a child. It is a part of your true and original self. And then you spend the rest of your life trying to get it back.

EPILOGUE

March 2012

We will not be thinking the unthinkable: Ryan Doumit is off to Minnesota. The Fantastic Ronny C won't be back, either. Apparently, the Bucs did not think he was quite as fantastic as I did. Sadly, they were not able to talk Derrek Lee into coming back, and Paul Maholm is gone too.

In their place, the Pirates picked up some players they hope will be a little better than the ones who left. Catcher Rod Barajas. Shortstop Clint Barmes. First baseman-third baseman Casey McGehee. Pitcher Eric Bedard. Nate McLouth was back too, making the Charlie Morton trade one for the good guys. The one pretty big money move the Pirates made, a trade with the Yankees for veteran pitcher A.J. Burnett, almost literally blew up in their face in the early days of spring training, when Burnett bunted a ball that broke an orbital bone in his eye socket that would cost him the first few weeks of the season.

These moves did not impress the experts much. Barring some big splash free agent, which will not be happening anytime soon, they will continue to pick the Bucs for the bottom or close until the Pirates prove they are better than that. I guess it's hard to argue after all these years. But it will make it that much sweeter someday when the Buccos prove them wrong.

****

I am back in the microfilm room of the Carnegie Library, doing the last bit of fact checking of this book. I have a feeling of contentment in this room that I can neither describe nor explain.

Most of the remaining facts are confirmed. Willie Stargell's home run over the roof at Forbes Field, the home run I did not get on film. Tommy Aaron's homer the next day, when my friend and I were almost tossed for throwing peanuts off the third deck, which did not make the paper.

As I always do, I learn something unexpected in the microfilm room. In the summer of 1971, from the middle of May through the middle of September, both newspapers, the *Pittsburgh Post-Gazette* and the *Pittsburgh Press*, were on strike. I had completely forgotten this. I know the essential facts here are right. You can get the basics from baseball-reference.com. But the best parts don't show up in the box score, and they may not have made the paper anyway. Like the day they gave Roberto Clemente three standing ovations in five minutes. Maybe there is an old radio broadcast somewhere. Otherwise, you will have to rely on the memories of me and anyone else who was there, and to know that if it is not exactly right, it's very close, and that I did my best.

****

Life is perfect. It is 85 degrees and we are in Bradenton, Florida for spring training, a birthday gift with this book in mind from Andee and the kids. Four games in four days at beautiful little McKechnie Field, named for Bill McKechnie, manager of the World Champion Pirates of 1925.

This was to be the first real vacation that Andee and I have taken together since the kids were born, which is now almost twenty-eight years ago, although, happily, it did not turn out that way. Our children live in New York, Chicago and College Station, Texas. They are where they are supposed to be and I miss them all the time.

****

The Pirates make a big move after all. The biggest move they have made in a long time. The Pirates sign Andrew McCutchen to a long-term contract. This is a statement. A vote of confidence. A reason to believe.

It is springtime in Pittsburgh and Pirate fans are filled with hope.

ACKNOWLEDGEMENTS

This is a book about baseball and family, or about family and baseball. It would not have been written without my family; there would have been no reason to write it. Andee, Lauren, Rachel and David have contributed to this book in more ways than I could ever explain. If you have made it this far, I think you understand.

I grew up in another family and this book also is about them. My parents, Amy and Frank Lowenstein, celebrated their sixtieth anniversary this year. They have taught me about holding together through good times and bad, and about what is important and what is not. My sister Peggy, whom I can always count on, and with whom I have a shared experience that only brothers and sisters can have. And Bill, who continues to set a very high bar.

To my in-laws, Estelle and Melvin Mann, who will be celebrating their fifty-fifth anniversary this year. They treated me like family from the very beginning and have been family for nearly thirty years.

To my extended family, especially my Uncle Stanley Levine and his son-in-law Marc Brown, the true keepers, along with my dad, of the Pirate flame and, in Marc's case, for the ticket group that got me back into this.

To all of the friends who sat with us in Section 22, most of all my baseball guide Jim Whalen, who sees things that other people don't, especially me. And to the many friends who took the time to read an advance draft of this book, and for their helpful suggestions.

To my friend and incredibly careful editor, Theresa Doerfler, who patiently learned or at least re-learned another sport as, once again, we tried to make this book the best that it could be.

To Tom Costello and all my friends at Word Association Publishing. It was great to get the band back together. With a couple new members too, Jason Price, a gifted designer, and Sherry Frazier, who is diligently spreading the word to the multitudes who would enjoy this book.

To Linda Parker and Steve Spolar at the *Pittsburgh Post-Gazette*, and to the Pittsburgh Pirates, for their thoughtful and professional help in gathering the photographs for this book.

To the Pirates of my childhood and the Pirates of today.

In the end, I am back full circle:

To Andee. For everything.

PHOTO CREDITS

Thanks to *The Pittsburgh Post-Gazette*, The Pittsburgh Pirates and Getty Images for the following photographs:

Copyright ©, *Pittsburgh Post-Gazette*, 2012, all rights reserved. Reprinted with permission. This copyright notice applies to each of the following photographs: PNC Park (front cover); Andrew McCutchen (p.55); Neil Walker (p.57); Jose Tabata (p.126); Neil Walker (p.126); Pedro Alvarez (p.127); Garrett Jones (p.127); Ryan Doumit (p.128); Ronnie Cedeno (p.128); Jeff Karstens (p.129); Charlie Morton (p.129); Paul Maholm (p.129); James McDonald (p.129); Kevin Correia (p.129); Alex Presley (p.130); Brad Lincoln (p.130); Derrek Lee (p.130); Joel Hanrahan and Michael McKenry (p.131); Clint Hurdle (p. 133); Joel Hanrahan (p. 135); Manny Sanguillen (p. 185); Bill Mazeroski home run (p.195); Roberto Clemente (p.198); Jeff Karstens (p.237); Andrew McCutchen (back cover).

Copyright ©, Pittsburgh Pirates, 2012, all rights reserved. Reprinted with permission. This copyright notice applies to each of the following photographs: Steve Blass (p.87); Pittsburgh Pirates 2011 Team Picture (p.125); Andrew McCutchen home run celebration (p. 132); Pittsburgh Pirates 1971 Team Picture (181); Roberto Clemente (p.182); Willie

Stargell (p. 183); Al Oliver (p. 184); Richie Hebner (p.184); Bob Robertson (p.185); Dave Cash (p.186); Rennie Stennett (p.186); Jackie Hernandez (p.186); Bob Prince (p.187); Dock Ellis (p.190); Bob Veale (p.191); Dave Giusti (p.191); Bruce Kison (p.192); Nelson Briles (p.192); Don Hoak (p.193); Dick Groat (p.193); Dave Parker (p.194); Barry Bonds (p.194); Honus Wagner (p.196); 1971 World Series (Steve Blass and Bob Robertson) (p.197); 1979 World Series (Willie Stargell) (p.197); Roberto Clemente (p.201); Willie Stargell (p. 265).

CHAPTER PHOTOS:

Part I: Heartbreak:

Sid Bream slides in safe at home.

Part II:

Andrew McCutchen

April:

Neil Walker

May:

Steve Blass

June:

Joel Hanrahan

July:

Roberto Clemente

August:

Jeff Karstens

September:

Willie Stargell

WA

Made in the USA
Monee, IL
19 October 2026

66035052R00177